Look In Amber

David Goodman

The Parrs Wood Press
Manchester

First Published 2005

THE PARRS WOOD PRESS
St Wilfrid's Enterprise Centre
Royce Road, Manchester, M15 5BJ
www.parrswoodpress.com

© David Goodman 2005

ISBN: 1 903158 71 0

Printed in Malta by Gutenberg Press

CONTENTS

INTRODUCTION

There is no definite starting point for *Look Back in Amber*, essentially as I can't remember my first game. I remember hating it and crying when City scored in a desperate and confusing attempt to persuade my grandfather to take me back home, but it was almost certainly at the beginning of the 1971-72 season. I think also that my first home game was Chris Chilton's last. I don't know what possessed my granddad to keep taking me but he did and after another couple of games of tears and sulking, I was completely hooked. Thirty-three years later I'm still hooked, though the sulking, which never disappeared, is if City lose rather than win.

My earliest football memory was the Stoke City FA Cup quarter-final in 1971. Over 40,000 packed into Boothferry Park to see the Tigers go two goals up only to see a suspect defence fail to keep Stoke at bay. I was a small boy at the time but remember my dad and granddad leaving my grandparents' house in North Road and returning having failed to see City reach the cup semi-finals. In those early years I used to sit on the sofa in the sitting room of their house and watch the crowds go by, a mass of people. If they were going left they were heading for Bunkers Hill and the South Stand seats. If they were heading right, it was to all other parts of the ground.

Their house was a wonderful place to visit for a boy who had become a City fan. Their spare room upstairs offered a glimpse of a few seats at the very top right-hand corner of the South Stand and the back garden was dominated by a view of the back of the Best Stand. A floodlight pylon stood at the end of the 'tenfoot'. The ground with its rusty green corrugated iron dominated the landscape for that terrace of houses on North Road between the Best Stand entrance and the entrance to the South Stand.

In the kitchen of the house, on matchdays, you could see one or two brave people climbing up the ladder to get to the television gantry and as kick-off approached you could hear the music playing over the tannoy, the comforting, yet supremely professional voice of Tom Drury and the *Match of the Day* theme which just preceded the teams coming out onto the field.

LOOK BACK IN AMBER

I was at their house once, during the mid-Seventies, and, having had flu, tried to persuade them to let me go to a home game against Middlesbrough, who were top of the division and led at that time by Jack Charlton. They didn't let me, so I had to endure the awful situation of being just yards away from where the match was taking place but having little idea of what was happening. I could see the people in the South Stand seats and hear the occasional noises coming from the game and, I think, managed to get into the ground for the last 10 minutes or so.

The memories I had, going to Boothferry Park in the early Seventies, was the size of the crowds, the atmosphere building up inside the ground and the excitement caused by a team still with ambitions of promotion to the First Division. Even at such an early age I remember being proud of the club, feeling that the ground was superb and that this was a big club, bigger than most of the teams that used to visit us on a Saturday afternoon.

Much has happened since those times in the early Seventies, but in some ways so little. Hull City has turned full circle and is back where it all started for me, as a big club playing in a great stadium in front of big crowds. We may have had some interesting times along the way but for youngsters starting to watch the club today, they'll be experiencing some of the same feelings that I did in 1971. Throughout all the turmoil, all the ridicule that the club has faced, I never lost my belief that this club had the potential to become 'big' again. Unlike some, I'm delighted to see the 'new fans' who have come to see City in the last few years and I've got no desire to go back to the 4,000 we used to get in the mid-90s, but there is a smug satisfaction I get in knowing that I'm a 'real' fan who has been through the hard times in order to appreciate the new era at Hull City.

There is no definite starting point to the book and no definite end. In some ways I've glossed over the Adam Pearson era as it is 'work in progress'. The rise of the club during his time in charge deserves a book of its own, perhaps to explain it more fully than I could do justice to here. It's a great story and, writing this after promotion has been confirmed back to what used to be called the 'Second Division', it's a wonderfully exciting time to be a follower of this club.

INTRODUCTION

The reasons for starting this book in 1971 was partly because that's when I started going to Boothferry Park but also because I think that the Taylor/Pearson era, which will hopefully last for many years yet, consigns the Wagstaff/Chilton era to the history books. Nobody who was there during the 1965-66 season, or the 1970-71 season to some extent, will ever forget that time. The names of Wagstaff, Chilton, Butler and Houghton will always be part of Hull City folklore, but time has moved on and with so many 'new' City fans around, the name Cliff Britton means as much to them as Ambrose Langley (City's first manager) means to me.

It is also worth noting that the 1960s have been written about with both Wagstaff and Chilton publishing their autobiographies but there has been nothing about the thirty years since then, despite all the lock-outs, the receiverships and the management changes that have affected the club.

I wouldn't claim that this is a comprehensive guide to all that went on at Hull City from 1971 to the present day. It's too vast a topic and, if I'd had my time again, I may have chopped ten years off to perhaps concentrate in more detail on 1981 to the present day. However, whatever the faults of the book, I hope and believe it to be a worthwhile work on Hull City during those years.

I owe many people a debt of gratitude for making this book possible. First of all, Adam Pearson for granting the book the club's approval but I should also thank Rob Smith, Marketing Manager at City, who has been my point of contact throughout. He has always been very enthusiastic about the project and was very helpful in getting me in touch with some of the club's former players, managers, chairmen and other members of staff.

My grateful thanks also to John Hawley, John Cooper, Garreth Roberts, Bruce Bannister, Martin Fish, Tom Wilson, John Cooper, Jeff Radcliffe, Don Robinson, Ken Houghton, John Kaye and Rob Smith again for the interviews they granted me. It was such a pleasure to meet all of them and all were very helpful. The book undoubtedly benefits from all of their contributions and it was a great pleasure to meet all of them. I am only sorry that I did not have chance to contact more people. Only starting work on the book in January 2005 meant that time was limited and I had to cut down on the number of people I got in touch with.

Thanks also to Stephen Fairhurst for providing me with some scrapbooks which came in very handy towards the end of my time on this book.

I'm grateful also to Andy Metcalf, Rich Lusmore and Gary Hook, one of whom thought up the title to this book. It was, of course, a fanzine, produced by the three of them in the early Nineties and, despite trying mighty hard, I couldn't improve on it. Thanks to them for their permission in using the inspired title for my book.

I should also thank my late grandfather for introducing me to Hull City and my dad also. He's been a Grimsby Town fan for about sixty years and is still as passionate about them today as ever. Apart from my fortnightly trips to Boothferry Park in the early Seventies, my dad used to drag me across the Humber now and again to watch the Mariners and my first visit to places like the Shay, Saltergate and Leeds Road was with my dad, following Town.

Not many City fans have the Mariners as their 'second team' but I am proud to and some of my best football memories have been at Blundell Park, such as seeing Town beat Everton in the League Cup and beating Exeter to clinch automatic promotion under Alan Buckley. Town have also come full circle since 1971, spending more seasons in the second tier, now the Championship, than elsewhere, but now they're back in the bottom division, hopefully not for long.

I thank all my family for the interest they have shown in this book. My mum, dad and Antony have taken a great interest and the research and writing has taken me away from Julie, Daniel and Jonathan for long periods, though it's been a great excuse when I felt like being on my own!

I have always remembered a car sticker that City used to sell in the early Seventies which said simply, 'Hull City: my club, my

INTRODUCTION

town, my team'. I haven't lived in Hull for over twenty years, longer than the amount of time I spent in the city, yet one thing remains constant; Hull is still my city and Hull City is still my club. I've always been quite proud of that.

PART ONE

Pushing for the top

Season 1971-72

The 1970-71 season so nearly saw City rid themselves of the 'biggest club never to have played in the first division' tag, which has always been a huge millstone around the club's neck. Three days after the demoralising defeat to Stoke in the FA Cup quarter-final, City looked to have put it behind them when they went, along with thousands of travelling fans, to promotion rivals Sheffield United. Goals from Simpkin and Wagstaff saw City win 2-1 to send the team to the top of the Second Division and promotion was on the horizon, but a disastrous Easter period saw City drop too many points to stay in contention and they eventually finished a disappointing fifth.

So the start of the 1971-72 season saw the Tigers attempt to put the previous season's disappointment behind them and take another tilt towards the big time. Cliff Britton, the manager of the 1965-66 Third Division championship side, who moved upstairs to become general manager after Terry Neill was appointed, decided to leave the club. Other changes saw Tommy Docherty appointed as the club's assistant manager and Tommy Cavanagh became reserve team coach, replacing John McSeveney who was sacked by the club after a 10-year association with the Tigers.

Docherty, early in his managerial career, was to last barely half a season at Boothferry Park. Soon after coming to Hull he was invited to take caretaker charge of the Scottish national side and was eventually offered the job as manager of Scotland on a full-time basis. He was replaced by Wilf Dixon, who came to Boothferry Park from Everton. This led to a further backroom reshuffle with Tommy Cavanagh moving up to work with the first team and Andy Davidson taking charge of the reserves.

Meanwhile, City's player-manager Terry Neill was appointed as player-manager of Northern Ireland, replacing Billy Bingham who had taken over the Greek national side. Neill had been concerned about the possible conflict in roles but City chairman Harold Needler persuaded him to take the job, saying that the role was a great honour for Neill and the club. He added that with the backroom staff in place the two roles shouldn't clash.

LOOK BACK IN AMBER

City lost at Charlton in the first game of the new season but then beat Oxford at home in a game which proved to be Chris Chilton's last as a Tiger. Speculation had grown about Chilton's role at the club when he refused to go on a pre-season tour of Sweden, leading to a fall-out between him and Neill.

Chilton had also refused to sign a new contract which alerted clubs including Coventry, QPR, Millwall, Chelsea, Sheffield Wednesday and Huddersfield who were all interested in signing the player. Huddersfield offered Jimmy McGill in exchange but Coventry were always the favourites and after talks at Highfield Road, Chilton decided on the move for a fee of £92,000.

Fortunately the Tigers already had a quality replacement in the emerging Stuart Pearson, who had made his debut in 1970 and was ready to become a first team regular. In 1965, when Pearson's father was painting the Boothferry Park stands, he told John Simpson, City's then assistant trainer, that he would give the club a gallon of paint if City would give his son, who had just left school, a trial. Simpson said that he would, without the paint, and Pearson embarked on a fruitful career, beginning at City but eventually leading to international caps with England.

Despite Chilton's departure, the team which had stayed together for a good few years, dominated by the forward line of Waggy, Chillo, Houghton and Butler, was largely still in place, though several others were reaching the end of their careers. Wagstaff was getting towards his twilight years as a force and Houghton and Butler were also coming towards the end of their time in black and amber.

Ken Houghton regretted the loss of Chilton. He said: '*When Chillo left we had an able deputy in Pearson but it still wasn't the same because they were different players. Pancho gave you a bit of everything but he couldn't deliver what Chillo gave you in the air. Nobody could.*'

Following the departure of Chilton, Wagstaff had talks with Terry Neill about his future at the club as he was thought to be unhappy with his role in the team and was unsettled by reports that the Tigers were chasing Bruce Rioch of Aston Villa. Villa were themselves interested in City's Chris Simpkin and an exchange deal involving the two players was mooted.

PUSHING FOR THE TOP

However, Simpkin signed for Blackpool for £30,000, money which was expected to be going towards the £70,000 fee that Liverpool were wanting for winger Peter Thompson, a player who had interested Neill for some time. One player who did arrive at Boothferry Park was Jimmy McGill, who signed for the Tigers from Huddersfield for £53,000.

At the same time City also made a bid for Martin O'Neill, a striker who had made a big impact in the Northern Irish League at Distillery. City bid £22,000 for the player who had recently won his first international cap but their interest cooled after the Irish club held out for more money. It proved to be the wrong decision as the player signed for Nottingham Forest and eventually went on to share in their championship and European Cup glory.

City were also on the lookout for a goalkeeper as they had been worried for some time about the lack of cover for Ian McKechnie and the club made enquiries about two keepers who went on to greater things. Partick Thistle turned down a City offer of about £50,000 for their 19-year-old keeper Alan Rough who had just won his first cap for the Scottish national side, and City were also closely linked with David Harvey who had been on the transfer list at Leeds United. However, City eventually settled on Darlington's 21-year-old keeper Jeff Wealands, who moved to Boothferry Park for £10,000, and City also signed John Kaye for £25,000 from West Bromwich to add steel to the defence.

Kaye remembers signing for the Tigers: '*Terry Neill was a good manager for City at the time. I knew him from playing in my West Brom days when he was with Arsenal. He was short of a centre-back so brought me into the club. West Brom initially said they'd let me go on a free but then changed their mind and said they wanted money for me.*

'*I didn't know many of the players when I got here. I think the only one was Chris Chilton because I'd played with him in the City A team many years before.*'

After the excitement of the previous campaign, the 1971-72 season was a disappointment with only a late rally, including a six-point Easter, allowing the Tigers to steer clear of relegation trouble, eventually finishing a relatively respectable twelfth. City benefited from the added grit, determination and leadership abilities that the likes of Kaye and McGill provided and the team also had the advantage of Bill Baxter's experience when he returned to Boothferry Park after being out on loan to Watford. Baxter ultimately played a major part in the club's end of season revival, forming a successful central defensive partnership with Terry Neill.

The disappointing league campaign was offset slightly by City's form in the cup competitions. City were drawn to play away at Norwich City who, at the time, were top of the Second Division with the Tigers second from bottom. However, City created a giant-killing of sorts by beating Norwich 3-0 with goals from Wagstaff, Butler and McGill.

This set City up for an intriguing visit to First Division Coventry City who of course had signed Chris Chilton from the Tigers earlier in the season. 2,000 City fans made the trip to Highfield Road and they were joined in the crowd by England manager Sir Alf Ramsey. Chilton led the Coventry team out onto the field but his new team-mates stood at the entrance to the tunnel to let Chilton take the applause from both sets of fans alone.

On a pitch which was recovering from a heavy snowfall, City scored the only goal of the game when a Frank Banks shot hit the inside of the post and Chillo's old partner, Waggy, was inevitably on hand to slot the ball home for his fourth goal in five games, putting City through to the Fifth Round for the second season in succession.

Ironically, after the cup win Coventry boss Noel Cantwell put Chris Chilton on the transfer list saying that the former Tiger had failed to settle in the Midlands with his play suffering as a result. City were interested in bringing him back to Boothferry Park but were put off by the £65,000 price tag and Chilton soon decided to retire from the game due to injury.

To reach the quarter-finals of the FA Cup, City would have to beat Stoke City in a repeat of the famous game of the previous season. City took about 4,000 supporters to the Potteries for the tie but this time the First Division team were never in danger and ran out 4-1 winners at the Victoria Ground, though City's plight in this game wasn't helped by an injury to Stuart Pearson, leaving John Kaye having to fill in as a makeshift forward.

As the season came to an end and City were clear of any lingering relegation worries, they hosted a friendly against Nacional Montevideo, the world club champions who had been Uruguayan champions four years in a row. A crowd of over 12,000 saw City go into a two goal lead through Stuart Pearson and John Kaye. Nacional came back to make the game all-square but City went on to score two more to win the game 4-2.

At the end of the season the manager sprung a surprise by giving a free transfer to Bill Baxter, whose return from the loan spell at Watford had been instrumental in City's rise up the table. Neill said that he was being released, along with five youngsters, so that the club could free up some money in order to make some new signings in time for the new season with Tommy Veitch of Hearts, Alex Pringle of Hibs and West Brom midfielder Bobby Hope heading Neill's shopping list.

Season 1972-73

By the beginning of the following season City had welcomed Phil Holme to the club in a bid to bolster the attack. Wilf Dixon was instrumental in bringing Holme to City, watching him play for Swansea on a number of occasions and, as a youngster at the club, John Hawley was impressed by the way that Neill used other people as part of his management team. He said: '*Terry Neill was great for me. He was top dog at Hull to some extent but he always got good people in to help him, such as Wilf, which in some ways he probably needed to. I played for Terry at Arsenal when he had Don Howe there which was a great combination because Terry was great off the pitch in PR and Don Howe was marvellous on the training pitch.*

'*A lot of people would have been scared to get the best coach probably in the world at the time but Terry was happy to do that and the combination at Arsenal of him and Don worked well together as it worked well with Terry and Wilf Dixon at City.*'

To add to the signing of Holme was the good news that Ken Wagstaff had re-signed for the club and would remain at City for the rest of his career. That was in contrast to Ian Butler, another of the famous forward line, who had been told by Terry Neill that he could leave the club. Butler claimed that the manager would not guarantee him a benefit in two years time despite him spending 10 years with the Tigers.

With hindsight, Ken Houghton feels that Terry Neill did change things around too quickly at the time:

'I thought that the team which had gone close in 1970-71 could have gone on for another couple of years and done really well but when a new manager comes into a side he wants to change things around and get his own players in. So, with hindsight I thought he disrupted the team. He felt he had to stamp his authority on the club, to change things and that's what happened.'

Of concern to Neill and the board as the new season crept nearer was the fact that crowds were down. An annual meeting at the beginning of the season gloomily pointed out that season ticket sales were falling as were attendances which had averaged over 20,000 during 1970-71 but had fallen to around the 12,000 mark a season later. It was feared that another disappointing campaign would see more empty spaces on the terraces and the five-figure crowds, which had become the norm for the best part of a decade, could become the exception.

Further evidence in the lack of support came when a pre-season game against Kaiserslauten, the West German cup finalists, attracted only 5,000 to Boothferry Park, a real disappointment to the board who had been hoping for a far larger gate for what they saw as an attractive friendly.

The *Hull Daily Mail* gave its viewpoint, putting most of the responsibility onto the product on the field. It said:

Attendances dropped drastically last season once it became clear that the hopes raised in 1970-71 were not to be realised and the fact that a year ago relatively poor sides could draw 6,000 more than a team coming from one of the world's top soccer nations is an unhappy omen. Only successful and attractive football will put that to rights and that means goals.

Goals had indeed been in short supply the season before with only 49 in 42 league matches and Neill was hoping that the signing of Holme would help spread the workload up front. City were still relying heavily on Ken Wagstaff to steer clear of injury and Stuart Pearson to continue his development. The pair had scored 26 of all league goals between them in the previous season so it was seen as vital to City's interests that they stayed both fit and in form.

With several in the first team coming towards the end of their careers, City were going to have to look towards youth and were fortunate that there were several youngsters who were showing themselves capable of adapting to first team football. Players such as John Hawley, Roy Greenwood, Jeff Hemmerman and Vince Grimes showed enough promise to suggest that the club's future, post-Waggy and Chillo, may still be bright.

Terry Neill was always looking to improve the squad and soon after the season started made a £40,000 bid for Coventry winger Quentin Young. He was hoping to recoup the money by selling Ian Butler, possibly to Oxford United, but the Young deal failed to come off with the player looking to regain his place in the Coventry first team and Butler decided to stay with City, at least in the short term.

City were also reported to be interested in other players including Manchester United and England legend Bobby Charlton. Neill confirmed that he had spoken to Frank O'Farrell, United's manager, about one or two players and that Charlton's name had been mentioned. However, it seemed unlikely that the move would ever happen as the former England captain had insisted that he wanted to end his career in the First Division and didn't want to drop down the leagues.

The 1972-73 season continued the trend of inconsistency which City had acquired, losing two of their first three games but then winning two in a row. A run of good form in September and October was followed by a poor November so there was never any suggestion that City were good enough to go up, or bad enough to go down. Whilst they appeared to have sorted out their goalscoring problem - Pearson got 17 and Holme 11 - some great wins such as the 5-1 win over Portsmouth, in which Pearson scored four, were negated by heavy defeats at Oxford and Burnley. In their defence

LOOK BACK IN AMBER

City were unlucky with injuries and Ken Wagstaff, crucially, was particularly affected, only being able to play in three matches before December.

John Kaye remembers: *'For me it was quite a good season as I was established in the team and I scored quite a few goals myself but the team just couldn't get a run going. There was no consistency which was a shame as we weren't far off being a good side.'*

City had a match against Nottingham Forest called off halfway through the season and hastily rearranged a friendly game away at Manchester United, with a crowd of 24,000 attending Old Trafford to see United win 2-1. However, the game was notable for seeing Tommy Cavanagh swap dugouts immediately after the final whistle. Tommy Docherty was the new United manager, about a year after leaving City, and he invited Cavanagh to join him at Old Trafford as coach.

By this time John Kaye had taken over from Ken Knighton as City's team captain. Terry Neill said that he had made the decision to give Knighton the chance to rediscover his form and regain his first team place, but his former captain gave a different interpretation saying that he couldn't properly represent the players as captain on the field while the manager was still playing. He added: *'At a team meeting the other day I put my head on the chopping block and voiced the opinions of a lot of the other players about Mr Neill's playing performances. Now I have felt the axe.'*

City at least ended the campaign on a high, beating Cardiff to secure a place in the following season's Watney Cup. City's 64 goals that season was the highest number of goals scored in the Second Division, except by those clubs which had been promoted.

Apart from the partnership upfront between Holme and Pearson, City had successes in defence with John Kaye having an excellent season and Frankie Banks playing in every game in every competition from the friendly with Kaiserslauten to Billy Wilkinson's testimonial match at the end of the season against West Ham.

PUSHING FOR THE TOP

It was another year which had seen City falter in the league but pick themselves up sufficiently to embark on another decent cup run. The Tigers beat Stockport after a replay to set up a tie against the mighty West Ham United, who included players of the calibre of Bobby Moore, Trevor Brooking, Clyde Best and Bryan 'Pop' Robson.

A crowd of 32,000, the biggest crowd since the Stoke City quarter-final, packed into Boothferry Park and saw the Tigers dominate the game against their First Division opponents, deservedly winning 1-0 after Pearson set up Ken Houghton to score the only goal of the game.

Houghton remembers: '*Everyone mentions the West Ham cup tie, but all I did was score the goal. Pancho did a great job on that, big Phil Holme did a great job, I was left just to stick the ball in the net. I always believe that the people who create goals should get credit as well.*'

Their opponents in the Fifth Round were Coventry City away in a repeat of the previous season's Fourth Round tie. The afternoon got off to a bad start when the City party had to go to Highfield Road in three groups after their bus broke down while outside their hotel on the outskirts of Coventry. It didn't improve when they got to the ground either as this time there was no giant-killing and the Tigers were beaten 3-0.

City also competed in the Anglo-Italian Cup and, drawn in the same group as Manchester United, Luton Town and Crystal Palace, the Tigers played Bari, Fiorentina, Verona and Lazio. Lazio were first to Boothferry Park and a crowd of over 7,000 saw a fiery game which City won 2-1 with goals from Ken Knighton and Roy Greenwood. Lazio at the time were top of the league in Italy but the game was remembered more for a fight on the pitch which flared up when one of the Italians floored Phil Holme. The resulting scrap led to City's assistant boss Wilf Dixon and substitute Ian McKechnie going out onto the pitch in a bid to calm the situation down.

As the season fizzled out, Neill was forced to deny that there had been offers for Stuart Pearson, Ken Wagstaff and Ken Knighton. It was thought that Sheffield United had been on the trail of Pearson and had turned to Wagstaff after an enquiry for Pearson was turned down by the Tigers. There were also reports that Sheffield Wednesday were looking at Ken Knighton.

City did make a signing of their own as the season ended. Scunthorpe United were said to have turned down a £50,000 offer from Manchester United for Steve Deere earlier in the season as they felt at the time they could get more money for him. However, the club's financial situation deteriorated and by the end of the season Deere had joined City for only £20,000, though Ken Houghton, a long-term Scunthorpe target, had gone in the other direction.

Ken Houghton remembers: '*The only reason I left City was because Terry Neill wanted Steve Deere from Scunthorpe and Ron Ashman, the Scunthorpe manager, said that, "The only way you will get Deere is if I can have Ken Houghton." I was happy at Hull, magic place and a really good professional set-up so I didn't want to go, but it's nice when somebody else wants your services.*

'*After a reserve game Wilf Dixon asked me to go into the office where Ron Ashman was sat. I again said I didn't want to go but Wilf got Terry Neill on the phone who was away with the Irish squad. He offered me an amount of money to leave, saying that he didn't want me to go which I didn't believe. So I told Ashman that I didn't want to leave Hull but because of the money and the fact that I wouldn't get in the Hull side the following season, I accepted Scunthorpe's offer.*

'*I went on holiday with my wife and kids and read in the paper that Ron Ashman had gone to Grimsby. I couldn't believe it and thought what have I done?! So I had a new manager who didn't know me from Adam, so it was probably the worst 12 months of my career though that wasn't Scunthorpe's fault, it was just circumstances.*'

Season 1973-74

At the beginning of season 1973-74 Terry Neill decided to retire from the game and concentrate on management, leaving a vacancy in the Tigers' central defence. Steve Deere had joined from Scunthorpe intent on forming a new central defensive partnership with John Kaye and there were other comings and goings before the new campaign got underway.

Ian Butler, another of the famous late Sixties/early Seventies team, finally left City to join York City for £10,000, whilst Ken Knighton also left Boothferry Park, joining Sheffield Wednesday for £60,000. Don Beardsley went to Grimsby Town but coming into the Tigers squad was Chris Galvin, brought in from Leeds United after being released by Don Revie to gain first team football elsewhere. Meanwhile Peter Daniel became a full-time professional at the age of 18.

After a bad start to the season, City were second from bottom after five games and Terry Neill looked again at possibly strengthening the side. He was hoping to sign Everton's Henry Newton and was prepared to pay between £70-80,000 which would have been a club record. He was also interested in Alex Reid, a Scottish international, who was playing for Newcastle United but both moves came to nothing.

City recovered from the appalling start and eventually finished in a respectable ninth position, though any hopes of a promotion charge were ended by an eight-game winless streak in December and January. Goals were a problem again with Stuart Pearson scoring eleven and Keith Wagstaff, despite playing in 32 league games, managing just eight.

The core of the side in 1973-74 included Deere and Roy Greenwood who both played in all 42 league games whilst Jeff Wealands, Stuart Pearson and Malcolm Lord missed just four games between them. Frank Banks, Roger DeVries, Jimmy McGill and Ken Wagstaff also played in the majority of games but thigh and cartilage injuries restricted John Kaye to just 18 league games and the loss of the inspirational Kaye was vital to City's season.

LOOK BACK IN AMBER

When Kaye ruptured his thigh muscle at Middlesbrough, Terry Neill briefly considered coming out of retirement but opted instead to sign Dennis Burnett from Millwall for a club record £60,000.

Halfway through the season City got knocked out of the FA Cup by Bristol City after a replay, a disappointment as City's chances of promotion also practically disappeared either side of Christmas and a run in the cup would have rekindled some interest. City would have faced West Ham again if they had got through to the Fourth Round.

However, City did have some success in the League Cup and after beating Leicester and Stockport, City were drawn at home to Liverpool in the fourth round. The game was played on a Tuesday afternoon at 2pm due to the power shortages that were brought about by the miners' dispute. City had looked at the possibility of playing the game under floodlights using a generator, as they were concerned at the attendance for a weekday afternoon fixture, but it was thought too risky, so the game had to kick off at 2pm. Played on a hard frosty pitch almost 20,000 managed to get to Boothferry Park for the game though most went home slightly disappointed after witnessing a poor goalless draw and Liverpool comfortably won the replay 3-1.

The gate that afternoon was comfortably the best of the season and with the team's mediocrity on the field, people were voting with their feet with the club only managing to attract three gates over 10,000 in the league.

City had at least managed to prolong the season beyond Christmas and even in March the fans were still clinging on to a faint hope of promotion with the team six points away from the promotion places. However, a defeat at home to Luton effectively ended any remaining hopes and City were left to plan for the following season.

Before the season ended, John Kaye was forced to retire with cartilage trouble, though he stayed at the club to help Terry Neill in a coaching capacity, and the campaign also saw the final appearance by Ian McKechnie who had been gradually displaced by Jeff Wealands in goal. He was released along with defenders Mel Green, Mike Connolly and forward Paul O'Riley. Phil Holme was forced to retire from the game following a long-standing knee injury but there was good news for the future with Dave Stewart, Ian Dobson, Dave Gibson and Paul Haigh, all aged 16, signing apprenticeship forms with the club.

Before pre-season training got underway, six City players including Roy Greenwood, Jimmy McGill, Jeff Wealands and Malcolm Lord, refused terms for the new season saying that the basic pay was unsuitable for the Second Division. However, after a lengthy dispute they all eventually agreed to new deals so City had a full and hopefully united squad going into the new season.

Season 1974-75

Soon after the 1973-74 season finished, Stuart Pearson left the club. The forward had helped the club forget the loss of Chris Chilton and had become a crucial figure for the Tigers, scoring 46 goals in 126 games. Pearson almost left for Manchester City towards the end of the previous season but a fee couldn't be agreed. A month later Manchester United came in for him and he left for Old Trafford with Peter Fletcher coming to City in exchange and the Tigers also receiving a fee of £200,000. It also meant that Pearson would potentially be playing against the Tigers during the season as United, famously, had been relegated through former hero Denis Law scoring against them for Man City. Few City fans begrudged Pearson the chance of a move as United were clearly 'on loan' to the Second Division and were strong favourites to go straight back up, though Pearson was the sort of player City needed if they were to make a promotion push.

The emphasis for the new season was a good mix of youth and experience. City had some older heads in the likes of Burnett, Lord, Deere, DeVries and Wagstaff but the overriding emphasis was on youth with Grimes, Hawley, Hemmerman and Greenwood all young and knocking on the first team door with several others in the reserves also looking for a call-up. Terry Neill said that if the side went out and played to its potential it would be an exciting season ahead. He also predicted that a lot of attention would be paid to 'the most promising crop of youngsters the club had had for many years'.

However, City made a poor start to the new season, winning just one of their first ten league games and were just off the bottom of the table when they were forced into a managerial reshuffle. Terry Neill had been disappointed to only receive a one-year contract renewal offer from City at the beginning of the season as he had been hoping for a longer deal, but he had failed to steer the club away from the slow but noticeable decline since the 1970-71 season brought City near to promotion and cup glory. Apparently the move from promotion chasers to mid-table stalwarts did not go unnoticed in the boardroom.

In September, just a few games into the new season, news came from North London that Bill Nicholson, Tottenham Hotspur's legendary manager, was to leave his post, creating a vacancy at one of the games most glamorous clubs. Johnny Giles, coming towards the end of his career at Leeds United, was the early favourite for the job but Terry Neill's name was also in the frame and as other candidates were ruled out for one reason or another, his was becoming the name most often mentioned in connection with the post.

Neill took charge of the Tigers in the 2-1 home defeat to Burnley in the League Cup in which Peter Fletcher scored his first goal since joining City, but immediately after the game City held a 45-minute board meeting and Spurs were told that they had permission to talk to the City manager.

He soon accepted an offer to take over at White Hart Lane and it was announced that his number two at Boothferry Park, Wilf Dixon, would prepare the City team for their next match, away to Nottingham Forest, before re-joining Neill as part of his management team at Spurs.

Harold Needler said: '*I can say that we are in a stronger financial position than when Terry took over and we have probably the best crop of youngsters in the club's history. Whoever does take over will have the benefit of that.*'

Needler was also quick to scotch rumours that Brian Clough would succeed Neill. Clough had been sacked by Leeds United after just 44 days in charge on the same day that Neill left Boothferry Park, but the City chairman stressed that the man who took Derby to Championship glory would not be coming to Hull.

John Kaye, already on the coaching staff at Boothferry Park, was invited to take over as caretaker manager on a four-match basis and came in at a crunch time for the club. City lost the Nottingham Forest game 4-0 and were too near the bottom of the table for comfort, having conceded 16 goals in just seven games.

Kaye said: *'I said that I would try it for a month to see if I got the respect of the players. I think after that month we'd only lost one game so I decided to have a go at it. I think we were second from bottom when I took over and we got into the top ten but couldn't get that final push.*

'I didn't find it hard to go from player onto the management side because I knew the players, I had the respect of the players and I think they appreciated the fact I was honest with them all. I told them that I wouldn't stand in anybody's way if they wanted to leave at any time to better their careers. I'd moved about myself on one or two occasions so I had to be straight with them.'

One of the first things Kaye did was put Roy Greenwood on the transfer list for a fee of £250,000. The player wanted First Division football and had wanted to get away from City for some time, turning down the offer of a new contract. Terry Neill, newly settled into the manager's seat at Spurs, was thought to have been the likeliest bidder for the player, obviously knowing him well, but the former City manager said he wasn't interested at that price. Greenwood's valuation eventually came down to £120,000 but there were still no takers and he eventually re-signed for the Tigers.

When Kaye took over his priority was to tighten a defence which had been leaking too many goals. Stuart Croft and Peter Daniel, two promising youngsters, were given their chance in the first team and City made an excellent signing in Dave Roberts from Oxford United for £75,000, who proved to be the sort of defensive leader that City had been lacking since Kaye himself had retired.

Kaye soon had the chance to test himself against the best when Manchester United came to town. Relegated the previous season,

LOOK BACK IN AMBER

United were favourites to go straight back up and had only lost two league games when they came to Boothferry Park in November with thousands of their fans taking over the whole of the East Stand and probably several hundred more in other areas of the ground.

In a bruising game, City ran out 2-0 winners with Lord and Wagstaff scoring the goals in front of 23,000. The *Yorkshire Post* reported on the game the following Monday, and said of City:

There was a feeling within football circles that the club's ambition had outstripped achievement for almost a decade. The club, like the players, had long been held rather too classy for the Second Division yet irritatingly unable to prove it. However, the win over Manchester United saw that City may have more reason to be optimistic than usual.

It had found bite to complement its skill and it has also found Alf Wood to complement Wagstaff. The bite left Manchester United bloody and beaten, overcome by a plan which determined to be effective rather than attractive and had men with discipline to put it into practice.

City had defended for most of the match, often with nine men behind the ball but managed to hold out and Blampey, Croft and Wealands stood out in a good hard-working team performance. United's manager, Tommy Docherty, was less than complementary to his old team and said that City had no chance of being promoted:

'If they go on playing like that they won't have enough men left for a team by the end of the season. They'll all have appointments at Lancaster Gate every week.'

He said that it was the roughest game his side had been involved in so far, adding that he was surprised as he thought that the Tigers had a reputation as a good footballing side. He added, 'Today they just concentrated on stopping us playing and the referee had no control on City who were trying to provoke the United players.' Not surprisingly, Kaye disagreed and City celebrated a famous victory.

Alf Wood, who impressed in the Man United game, had only recently signed for the club from Millwall for a record £75,000. He chose the Tigers over West Brom and was on the motorway, on the point of turning off for Birmingham, when he decided to go up to

PUSHING FOR THE TOP

Hull to hear what John Kaye had to say. He didn't know where Hull was from the M1 so Kaye was forced to drive up to the motorway to meet him, only going on what car Wood was driving!

He was seen as a good buy for the club, being the type of player who could release others around him to create chances while he took the weight and responsibility, and it was hoped that when the injured players unavailable for the Man Utd game returned to action, City could mount a more realistic promotion challenge. The bookmakers agreed, slashing City's odds for promotion from 100-to-1 to 33-to-1 immediately after the Manchester United victory.

However, the game was something of a false dawn as 1974-75 ended as another season which had promised much but failed to deliver. After John Kaye was made manager in September, City went on a run, the Manchester United game included, which took them from fifth from bottom to fifth from top and by early December the team looked well capable of launching a sustained promotion push. Other notable results included beating Sunderland and Bristol City, who were in the top two or three all season.

However, when City needed to push on to get the results to cement their position near the top of the table, they could not manage to do it and in the two months just before and after Christmas, they slipped down the table and also lost out in the FA Cup to eventual finalists Fulham.

Kaye had achieved his initial aim which was to make City harder to beat. The defence had tightened up, but, from being renowned as a good footballing side who went out to entertain, City seemed to lose some of the creative and positive aspects of the game at the same time and the team appeared more concerned not to lose games than entertain during the second half of the season in particular.

In the team's defence, John Hawley was injured and out for two months, whilst the increasingly injury-prone Ken Wagstaff was out for about half the season. If both had been available for longer, perhaps things would have been different. Whatever the slight misgivings about the squad, under John Kaye the team had quickly moved away from relegation trouble and finished the season a creditable eighth and the new boss was popular with both players and supporters.

John Hawley enjoyed playing under Kaye: '*John was a wonderful man and a good manager. He wore his heart on his sleeve and you couldn't lie to John because he would never lie to you. I had a great working relationship with him, in fact everybody did. You certainly knew where you stood with John at all times.*'

Jeff Radcliffe, the club's physiotherapist, agreed: '*John was down to earth, a hard man who called a spade a spade. He was the same as a player, I remember him and Tommy Smith colliding when we played Liverpool at Boothferry and you could almost feel the stand rattle!*

'*His straight talking got him into trouble with the chairman. He used to ring John up and say sign so and so, he scores every couple of games, and John would reply that the same player had retired three years ago, now bugger off and leave me alone to sort the team out! When manager, he didn't like interference from above and wanted to run the team how he saw fit, which is how it should be.*'

Once the season ended, one of the club's rising stars, John Hawley, made a temporary move away from Hull, spending the summer playing for St Louis in the United States along with Dennis Burnett. He said:

'*I went to America for the summer and absolutely loved it. At the same time Dennis Burnett went from Hull to play for the same team. I could have stayed there and I did toy with the idea of doing that because I was an amateur and the club couldn't stop me. The lifestyle would have suited me down to the ground but I wanted to play in English football at as high a level as I could.*'

Season 1975-76

1975 marked the end of an era for City in many ways with the retirement of perhaps the club's best-ever player and two sad deaths. Cliff Britton, who had led the great team of 1965-66 and had stayed with the club in the early years of Terry Neill's time in charge, had died and a couple of months earlier, the death was announced of Harold Needler.

PUSHING FOR THE TOP

Needler, City's chairman and the man responsible for making the club, for a time, one of the biggest outside the First Division, passed away in July 1975 and his legacy was a Boothferry Park ground that was one of the best outside the First Division, largely because of the improvements that Needler himself had financed.

The seats and roof on top of Bunkers Hill, the new gymnasium and the six floodlights, all improved the ground significantly to the extent that it was used to host a Leeds v Spurs game when Leeds were banned from using their Elland Road ground, played host to England Under-21 games and also staged an international between Northern Ireland and Spain when Terry Neill was boss. However, the biggest regret for Needler was that the ground had never hosted regular First Division football and he died with that dream unfulfilled.

Harold's death left a huge gap in the boardroom though his replacement as chairman was his son Christopher, already a director. As a goodwill gesture, the new chairman took the unusual step of giving away a complimentary programme for the Bristol Rovers game in October 1975 which had a personal statement from Needler inside.

Added to the board had been Geoffrey Needler, Bob Chapman, Malcolm Kay and Trevor Thomas and Needler hoped that the new board would take the club on to greater success. He said: '*The new board members are aged between early thirties and late forties, and they have been chosen from different backgrounds and experiences to give us the Board structure and renewed vigour which I believe we need. I hope that with these hand-picked colleagues, and your support, I can guide John Kaye and his backroom staff into securing from the team, the end result which we all so keenly desire.*'

Sadly, the end result was dwindling crowds, a decaying stadium and the team plummeting down the league, but at the time it was designed to alleviate fears amongst City fans who had loved and respected 'Big Aitch'.

The first eleven for the Bristol game were Wealands, Banks, DeVries, Stewart, Croft, Roberts, Hawley, McGill, Wood, Wagstaff and Greenwood, a team that blended youth with experience and was looking to progress in the new season. However, by the time of the Bristol Rovers game, City had slid down the league after a good start of four wins in their first six matches. The Bristol game ended 0-0 in front of just five and a half thousand, which showed how the club had declined since the heady days of the late Sixties.

City never got back into the top half that season, though amid another frustrating campaign came some outstanding performances with an Easter thrashing of Oldham proving particularly memorable, with Peter Daniel looking outstanding at right back. However, the game following that was Sunderland at home which saw the Tigers outclassed and beaten 4-1.

Once again it was up front where the problems lay. It simply wasn't a side that was scoring enough goals to make an impact. Roy Greenwood and Alf Wood were our top scorers with six goals apiece which told its own story. The strikeforce seemed to be the weakest the team had fielded for some time and was all the more frustrating as supporters' memories of Chilton, Wagstaff and Pearson were still fresh. Indeed, this season saw Ken Wagstaff play his last game in the black and amber when, following a home victory over Portsmouth, he aggravated a long-standing knee injury and was forced to retire from the game.

Wagstaff had gone and Alf Wood had failed to make a positive impact whilst John Hawley was often playing more as a midfield player pushing forward. At least City's defence had improved with only 26 goals conceded in 21 away games, giving the side the best away defensive record since Terry Neill's first season in 1970-71. The defence was led by Wealands, Daniel and Croft who all had good seasons whilst Vince Grimes, Dave Gibson, Paul Haigh and Ian Dobson were added to the team and looked promising new additions.

John Kaye had appointed Jimmy McGill as club captain before the season started, thinking that he would provide the competitive spirit in midfield that the team needed, but he could not find his way back in the team after getting injured and was given a free transfer to Halifax Town in February 1976. Other departures saw Steve Deere joining Stockport County on loan before retiring from the game and Roy Greenwood finally got his wish to move away from Boothferry Park, moving to Sunderland for £140,000 a price which Kaye was happy with.

However, he argues that the Roy Greenwood sale was meant to provide him with funds which would have pushed City onto a higher level. He said: '*We sold Roy Greenwood to get us back in the black and I was intending to get three players that I'd been lining up, but in the end, once they had the money in the bank they wouldn't give it to me for the team and that's when it all started to go sour as far as I was concerned.*

'*It was unfortunate for us at that time because we'd lost Harold Needler. Christopher took over and he got one or two people on the board who weren't really in it for the football. They saw it as a joyride for publicity for themselves and started interfering.*'

However, Kaye did have enough money to afford Dave Sunley who was signed from Sheffield Wednesday for just £7,750. He had been valued at £150,000 at one time so City were hoping that they had a bargain, and City also bought in George Lyall from Nottingham Forest and Scottish winger Jimmy McIntosh, also from Forest for a small fee.

Season 1976-77

Before the 1976-77 season started, John Kaye was looking for two goalscorers, a full-back and an experienced midfielder with Alan Ball heading the shopping list. The Ball transfer had been close to going through the previous season with Arsenal interested in taking John Hawley in exchange, but Bertie Mee, the Arsenal manager, changed his mind and the deal was put on ice, though the City manager was hoping to go back to Arsenal with an offer once the season was underway.

Kaye's interest in Ball, a big-name player, was perhaps indicative of the fact that City were treading water, becoming a mediocre second division outfit, far removed from the side that entered the division 10 years previously. With Bristol City getting promotion and Portsmouth being relegated, City were now the longest-serving club in the Second Division and had lost momentum.

LOOK BACK IN AMBER

Kaye is adamant, however, that his plans for the club, with new signings, would have improved the side and made it into one capable of promotion. He said: '*I was looking at the likes of Frank Stapleton, Alan Ball, who I used to room with when I was with the England squad, and Terry McDermott. So I was looking at players like that who would have done well for the club but I couldn't get the backing of the board. They were all players who went on to prove themselves. Even Ball, when he left Arsenal to go to Southampton, would have been a good signing for us.*'

The team for the first game of the season, away at newly-promoted Hereford United, was Wealands in goal, Daniel and DeVries the full-backs, Croft and Roberts in central defence, Grimes, Haigh, Stewart and Lyall in midfield and Wood and Sunley up front.

A bruising game saw City lose 1-0 with John Kaye complaining that the opponents played like 'Hereford bulls'. It was a disappointing start that forced Kaye into making changes with several players injured in the Edgar Street game. Youngsters Gibson, Hemmerman and Hawley, who had just signed professional terms after several seasons as an amateur, came into the side and City beat Luton 3-1 the following Tuesday in a really professional display.

It was to get better when cup-holders Southampton came to town the following Saturday. The Saints had beaten Manchester United in the previous May's FA Cup Final and were favourites to get promotion at the end of the season.

Their front pair of Channon and Osgood may have seen better days but it was a test for the Tigers as to their own promotion credentials and it was a perfect afternoon as nearly 8,000 saw City win 4-0 with goals from Hawley, Stewart, Lyall and Sunley. Just as importantly, the football the team played that afternoon was sublime at times, outpassing and outplaying the cup-holders. Dave Stewart, aged just 18, was superb on the left wing and fully deserved his goal, with the other youngsters in the line-up - Gibson, Hawley, Daniel, Croft and Hemmerman - all playing well.

The national *Daily Mail*, following the Southampton game, gave the team this praise: *There is a small but significant band of soccer stars being reared at a Far East outpost on the soccer map... John Kaye's cubs. More accurately known as Hull City, they are a shining example to bigger clubs everywhere, a positive advertisement for everything that is good about the game.*

Sticking in the mind of a twelve-year-old boy that afternoon were the standing ovations given by the crowd to the team at half-time and full-time. I don't remember having seen them before this point and it was so good to see the crowd get behind the team and show their support at the end of the game.

The table that weekend looked wonderful. City were second in the table behind Chelsea and ahead of a number of other clubs also on four points. We may have only been three matches into the new season but it had begun well for the young Tigers.

City came back down to earth when losing to Orient in the League Cup before getting a decent away point at Carlisle with John Hawley equalising for the Tigers. City's first signing of the new season came on the eve of an away game at Bolton when Gordon Nisbet joined the Tigers from West Bromwich Albion. City lost that game 5-1 and after another draw, at home to a Sheffield United side containing Keith Edwards, City were heading back to mid-table after the early-season fun. It was also a side which had lost some experience in recent weeks. Alf Wood was injured in the first game at Hereford and centre-half Dave Roberts was expected to be out until at least Christmas after an operation on his back.

Kaye remembers: *'One of the biggest mistakes I made was at the start of that season when I put about six kids in all under 18 and we started the season wonderfully. But I thought that they can't keep it up and I was going to have to give them a rest. I did that and the team stopped playing. Looking back in hindsight, what I should have done was play them until they went off a bit and then give them a rest. I was trying to protect them a bit too much.'*

It was news off the field that was to reignite the feel-good feeling that had been absent from Boothferry Park for so long. Leeds United were still, arguably, the greatest force in English football at the time. Although they were trophy-less and the famous Don Revie side of the early 1970s was slowly breaking up, there were still some household names at Elland Road. The biggest of those names was the heartbeat of the side, one Billy Bremner. City had been linked with Bremner in the summer when it became clear that Alan Ball wouldn't be joining the club as City were still searching for an experienced face at the heart of an essentially young side, though few expected such a household name to arrive in Hull.

However, the talk about Bremner did not go away and it increased in the early weeks of the 1976-77 season. It was also speculated that a possible Bremner signing would not be the end of any comings and goings between City and Leeds. There were rumours that Leeds were interested in Dave Stewart, Pete Daniel and John Hawley whilst City were thought to be trailing Peter Lorimer, another Elland Road legend who was nearing the end of his career.

On Thursday September 23, 1976 came the news that City had been waiting for; Bremner had signed for the Tigers for £25,000 in a move which shocked the football world and perhaps signalled the club's intent to try and achieve the long-awaited dream of First Division football. It was hailed by Kaye himself as the most significant signing the club had made since those of Raich Carter and Ken Wagstaff many years before.

Kaye was aiming for the long awaited dream of the First Division and felt that Bremner could help provide it. He said: *I was honest with the players when he came. I said, "He's on more money than you lot but if we get promotion through his experience then you'll all get the same money," and they just accepted it.*

Bremner himself said of his new challenge: '*John Kaye sold this club to me very well. He convinced me that they are looking for success and I hope that I can be part of it. We have got some good young players here and I hope that my experience and influence can do a lot for the club.*'

The signing came too late for the following Saturday's game in which City earned a goalless draw at Burnley but, once that fixture was out the way, the stage was set for Bremner to make his Hull City debut at home to Nottingham Forest. A crowd of over 16,000, the biggest at Boothferry Park for some time, saw the slightly surreal sight of the former Scotland captain and Leeds United legend come out of the tunnel wearing the black and amber of Hull City.

PUSHING FOR THE TOP

The game was quite patchy with City perhaps a bit nervous with all the expectancy surrounding Bremner in the week leading up to the game. Jeff Hemmerman was the unluckiest man on the field, incredibly having four goals ruled out, but City took the points when a wonderful free-kick from Bremner, which he floated expertly over the Forest wall, ensured it was a dream debut.

City lost to Charlton in London's game of the day the following Saturday before beating Wolves 2-0 with goals from John Hawley, who had been pushed upfield at the expense of Dave Sunley. The game, which attracted 12,000, also saw the *Match of the Day* cameras pay a rare visit to Boothferry Park.

Kaye did not intend for Bremner to be the last of the new arrivals at Boothferry Park and he was in the market for others to aid what he hoped would be a promotion push. Rumours persisted that other members of the famous Revie side would also be moving to East Yorkshire. The Lorimer talk continued and another coming to the end of his career, Norman Hunter, was also linked with a move to Boothferry Park.

Kaye admitted that he was monitoring the situation at Elland Road though he was resigned to other teams also taking a close interest in Hunter. However, a player exchange was possible with Leeds scouts taking in most City games at this time. Daniel, Haigh and Hawley were all being tracked by the First Division club and would command six-figure fees. Kaye indeed confirmed that he had turned down a bid of over £100,000 for one of his stars.

In a bid to free up more money, City gave Alf Wood a free transfer, sold Gordon Staniforth to York for a fee in the region of £10,000 and loaned Chris Galvin to York for three months.

However, despite the conjecture there were no other signings and the euphoria over the Bremner signing soon abated. The inspirational performances against Luton and Southampton also became distant memories as the 1976-77 season was to become yet another without any promotion or relegation tension, or even any significant cup interest.

The season was not to become a promotion campaign as Kaye might have wished, but he does not regret the signing of Bremner. He said: '*Bremner was a great signing for us. The only thing was that he injured his back so we didn't get the best of him. The crowd went up to 16,000 for his first game for us, so what we paid for him we got it back in the first game.'*

The Tigers were overstaffed in midfield, a problem which Bremner's arrival exacerbated, but were short of quality up front. City had Sunley, Wood and Hemmerman as strikers with Hawley also able to play up front but the team were short of goals and a quality striker was essential if the club was to make a push for the top half of the table. Kaye himself knew that it was an issue and midway through the season City even looked at the possibility of bringing Ken Wagstaff back to the club, but any such move was vetoed by the Football League because he had already been paid disablement insurance.

Kaye was looking in many areas in a bid to improve the side and Jeff Radcliffe, City physio, believed in the manager's judgement. He said: *'He was a good manager and had an eye for decent players. We were looking at forwards and I remember John wanted to sign Frank Stapleton when he was a kid, I think Arsenal only wanted £40,000 or something like that, which would have been a great signing.'*

The Stapleton signing didn't happen but Kaye tried to ring the changes as best he could. Alf Wood left the club, joining from Middlesbrough, and Kaye brought in veteran John Hickton on loan from Middlesbrough, though there was never any prospect of the move being permanent. Sunley was suffering from the lack of a regular partner up front but Hickton's arrival prompted Sunley to score four goals in six games and the Middlesbrough striker himself scored a great goal to help City beat Carlisle. Hemmerman came back into the side after Hickton's departure but failed to make an impression and Rob Macdonald was also tried out before the season finished.

The situation up front was highlighted by the fact that Peter Daniel's six penalties scored that season made him the joint leading scorer. City looked at bringing in two strikers from St Mirren but the Saints manager, a young Alex Ferguson, insisted that the two, called Hyslop and Richardson were not for sale. Kaye also went back in for Alan Ball from Arsenal but again was unsuccessful.

PUSHING FOR THE TOP

Ultimately, City's season reached its high-point with the 16,000+ crowd to greet Bremner's debut but by the end of the season, City's last home game, a 2-1 defeat to Cardiff City, was played out in front of just 3,500, the club's lowest ever Second Division crowd at the time.

The club was in a vicious circle as there was little money to bring in a quality forward and crowds were down and getting lower because the football was not getting any better. There appeared no solution to the problem, short of the club finding another gem in the juniors or speculating to accumulate, but with Harold Needler gone, the prospects of that were remote. It was already apparent that City would struggle the following season unless a striker capable of scoring at least a dozen goals could be found.

As the end of the 1976-77 season approached, three players were released: Grahame McGifford, winger Jimmy McIntosh and striker Jeff Hemmerman. McGifford had never really had a chance to shine in the first team whilst McIntosh had flattered to deceive since signing from Nottingham Forest. City was a chance for him to resurrect his football career and despite a promising first couple of games, he rarely looked like the answer on the wing. Hemmerman on the other hand, had been a promising youngster at City for several years and perhaps suffered through coming into the side while peoples' memories were still full of Chilton, Wagstaff and Pearson.

It looked a hasty decision to release him with so little else up front and Hemmerman showed City what they were missing by continuing in league football for several years, doing well at Portsmouth and Cardiff, scoring 22 goals in Cardiff's promotion campaign of 1982-83.

PART TWO

Slide down the leagues

Season 1977-78

As the new season approached, rumours of which striker City were poised to sign became practically a nightly event. Duncan McKenzie of Everton was one of the targets and the manager was reportedly so keen to bring in a quality striker that he was again prepared to offload one of his number of saleable defenders; Croft, Daniel or Haigh would all have brought in a significant fee if sold.

McKenzie never arrived at Boothferry Park but City did sign Bruce Bannister from Plymouth Argyle for £15,000 after the forward had made his name in the 'smash and grab' partnership with Alan Warboys at Bristol Rovers.

Bruce remembers signing for City. He said: '*We'd just bought a house in Plymouth after we'd been staying at the Holiday Inn on the Hoe in Plymouth for four months. My wife had literally finished putting up the last curtains when Hull came in for me!*'

It was an advantage that Bannister knew John Kaye. He even claimed to have learnt from him as a player. He said: '*I'd only ever bumped into John Kaye as a player once and that was when he was at West Brom and I played against him whilst I was at Bradford City. He was a good player; he was solid as a rock and quick for a defender. My job was to mark him when he came forward. So a corner comes in and he turns to me and says, "I'm going to come through you". I say, "Well, we'll see about that." But it had an effect because after that I was watching him rather than the ball and they could have scored.*

'*It always had an effect on me and I used the phrase myself in a game prior to my move to Bristol. It was to one of the Bristol Rovers players who'd just kicked me and I said to him, "I'm coming through you." The ball came across, he was watching me instead of the ball and I scored. So I'd learnt something from John.*

'*John was instrumental in me signing for Hull because I knew that he was a good professional and I liked his honesty. When you meet him it comes out in him blatantly. He calls a spade a spade and I like that. He said to me just before I signed that Spurs were also wanting to talk to me, they had just been relegated to the*

Second Division. But he had the City contract in his hand and I said that I would sign it. I think that was naivety on my part because Spurs were the bigger club but I saw the move to Hull as a move back to Yorkshire, which suited me at that time in my career and I knew about the club and its potential.'

He was also attracted by the coaching side which saw Kaye involved himself along with the redoubtable Andy Davidson and the newly-appointed Bobby Collins.

Before the season started, pressure increased on the side to get off to a successful start with news that one or two of the City regulars were unsettled. Jeff Wealands felt that it was now or never if he was to play in the First Division and Peter Daniel and Dave Roberts also expressed a desire to play at a higher level. So when City kicked off the new season, John Kaye knew he had to deliver.

The manager had the added problem of eight players in dispute with the club over pay. The rebels - Dobson, Croft, Daniel, Wealands, Blackburn, Gibson, Grimes and Stewart - all took their cases to an independent tribunal and though all eventually reached agreement, it had an unsettling effect on the squad in the opening weeks of the season.

The opening day was a great success with the Tigers beating Sunderland 3-0 in front of over 16,000 at Boothferry Park. It was to be the highest crowd of the season, boosted of course by the large support from Wearside who took over the whole of the East Stand. City lost away to Sheffield United but then won at Crystal Palace to complete a satisfactory first couple of weeks.

On paper the Tigers looked to have a side well capable of surviving in the Second Division. The established names of Bremner, Roberts, Wealands, Lord and DeVries were joined in the first team by some of the best youngsters the club had developed in years but though the season had started relatively well, the team were not still not scoring enough goals.

Alan Warboys was signed from Fulham for £25,000 to re-form the Warboys-Bannister partnership which had served Bristol Rovers so well, but it was not working in Hull and the team were in mid-table when Mansfield came to town and went away with a 2-0 win in a terrible game for City. It was the last straw for the directors and John Kaye was dismissed at 5.35 on the Saturday afternoon just over half an hour after a game in which only Dobson, Galvin and Roberts emerged with any credit.

It was a shock to the supporters but Christopher Needler said that he had been considering whether to change the manager for some time and added that it would have needed the team to have won very convincingly for him to change his mind over the decision to sack Kaye.

He said: '*It has been terribly difficult, terribly hard but we told John we were not happy with the situation at the start of the season and gave him two months to produce the goods. Those two months expired and unfortunately we are no further on. John has had three years almost to the day of complete control of the team and no interference from me.*'

Kaye admitted that he had failed to provide enough in the three years he had been in charge. Judging by what happened to the club in the following years, that was debatable, but he had nevertheless become the first manager that City had sacked in 20 years, something that made the decision to part company even more difficult for Needler.

It was a sad moment for those players who had been attracted to the club by Kaye himself and most supporters felt that the timing of the decision, when the club was in a relatively healthy position in the Second Division, was a strange one.

Jeff Radcliffe said: '*At the time he was sacked we were quite high up the league but I think his attitude towards the board didn't help him in the end. I think that the board had got fed up of John mouthing off at them.*'

Ken Houghton believes it led to problems the club was to encounter in later years: '*I remember John coming in and saying to me before the Mansfield game, "If we don't win today I'm going to get sacked." We'd had a few bad results but that happens and we got beat by Mansfield. That starts a slippery slope because when a club starts changing managers left right and centre they're going to be in trouble and that's what happened. If City had stuck with Yorkie I don't think the club would have been in the position it found itself in.*'

LOOK BACK IN AMBER

After his sacking, Kaye revealed that he had the chance to go back to West Bromwich Albion as manager in the summer but had turned it down because he felt that City had great potential.

Kaye said: *'I thought when they got rid of me that we weren't far off being a side capable of challenging for promotion. If we'd have got the players I wanted I think we'd definitely have been in with a shout. We had some good players there at the time but they just wanted somebody to stabilise them like Ball or McDermott and someone to score goals. We'd lost Pearson and Waggy and they're players who took some replacing.*

'One mistake I did make was in buying a couple of players based on past experience. I got one who I should never have signed. One forward who came here should have been a great signing because when he was at his previous club he created things for other players but it didn't work out here. I made the mistake of going on his past reputation and I didn't go for a final look at him to make my own mind up.'

The chairman immediately appointed Bobby Collins who Kaye had brought to the club in July as caretaker and asked Andy Davidson to stay on as coach while the club advertised the manager's job. Needler said he would consider everyone for the post including Billy Bremner, who was the subject of most of the press speculation. Bremner, along with Dave Roberts, had been the first player to see Kaye, after his sacking and he appeared to genuinely feel for Kaye.

He said: *'At the moment I'm so disappointed for John that I can't really think about anything else. I will need a few days to sort myself out.'*

John Kaye remembers: *'I was surprised that Bremner didn't get the job but I think that he had a lot of respect for me in the same way that I had for him. We'd played against one another many times when he was at Leeds and we both had the same passion for the game. We both badly wanted to win and I think that he was a bit upset when I left along with some of the other players.'*

Most City supporters thought that Billy Bremner was a shoe-in for the job and it was a feeling that had some grounds, according to the views in the dressing room.

SLIDE DOWN THE LEAGUES

John Hawley said: '*Billy Bremner should have been the manager when John left. He was offered the job but out of loyalty to John he turned it down because he felt it would be disrespectful. So then they turned to Bobby Collins, who had been John's assistant. Collins said yes and the deal I think was that Billy was going to take over in time but I think they had a big fall out at that point.*'

Bruce Bannister remembered the period in a similar way: '*For some reason Billy didn't want to be seen to stab John in the back, so that's why it didn't happen. I think what should have happened was that Billy should have been sorted before John. Someone should have sounded him out and said to him that John was going to have to leave and would you take over if he did. If they'd have done that they would have known exactly where they stood. In all probability they would have had the same answer because Billy was a straight guy, a lovely man.*'

For Bannister, Bremner taking over would have been a natural progression for the man who was already a leader on the pitch. He remembers: '*During this period my father died and I came over to Bradford to live with my mum for a while so I travelled for maybe a month through to Hull. I met Billy and Alan Warboys at the A1 and then Billy drove us in to Hull. We did it that way rather than bringing three cars. So I got to know Billy quite well.*

'*He was a leader in the dressing room and was a bubbly character but his football life had always been at the top of the game captaining Scotland and Leeds United in their heyday. If you are preparing someone to face Manchester United at Old Trafford in front of 70,000 you bring people down a bit because people are so hyped up anyway. Billy was good at taking the pressure off folk whereas if you are playing in front of four men and a dog you need picking up and he wasn't really used to being in a dressing room that needed picking up.*

'*However, people listened to what he had to say. If someone tells you you did something well, you just think well, what does he know? But if Billy told you then you listened. He was the star player at the time and his vision and ability were wonderful.*'

LOOK BACK IN AMBER

Though the dressing room may have wanted Bremner to be the next manager, it appeared that the board had other ideas. It was rumoured that they doubted whether Bremner had the right credentials to be manager of the club and were said to have felt snubbed when he rejected the chance to become coach when Phil Holme left the club.

Another train of thought was that the two of them would team up to form a management partnership. Though they were also seen as rivals for the job, the fact that they had worked so well together at Leeds United led many to think that a partnership between the two of them would have been beneficial to City.

Indeed, when Bremner signed for the Tigers, he said, 'If I can do as good a job for Hull City as Bobby Collins did for Leeds United ten years ago then I'll be satisfied.' However, for whatever reasons, Bremner continued as a player and Collins was his caretaker manager.

The following Wednesday, City had a perfect start to life after Kaye when Spurs came to Boothferry Park as holders of one of only three remaining unbeaten records in the league. They were also firm favourites for promotion straight back to the First Division which they had left just the previous May.

Bremner was sat in the stands with a heavy cold that night but he saw his team-mates record a surprising and excellent victory to kick-start their season with Alan Warboys scoring two magnificent goals in a five-minute spell in the first half. This result, combined with a draw at Millwall and a victory over Blackpool, was enough to persuade the directors to hand the job to Collins on a permanent basis after a 17-day period as caretaker. The new manager kept Andy Davidson as assistant manager and Ken Houghton came back to the club as youth team coach.

Collins was a popular choice with the supporters. His flair for leadership was proven at Leeds where he had authority over a young team and he was seen as a man with the leadership qualities, experience and ability to motivate players. This appeared to be evident from City's improved position in the league table and into November, City were healthily placed in mid-table looking up towards the promotion places rather than down towards the relegation spots.

SLIDE DOWN THE LEAGUES

Collins himself saw that there was a good future for the club with some good youngsters and experienced players and he saw his job as to build on what had been achieved over the three matches when he was in temporary charge and to convince people that it wasn't a flash in the pan. He said: *'When I look around Hull City I am convinced there is not a better job in the game than being manager here.'*

Bruce Bannister was another pleased with the appointment. He says: *'Bobby was a wonderful character. I've been in a charity dressing room with Norman Hunter and asked him who he was most afraid of and he said Bobby Collins in training! Everyone laughed because they all thought he was kidding but he wasn't. Bobby was an exceptionally hard man. He taught all the Leeds boys of the time what they knew. You talk about Giles being tough but Bobby was in a different league.*

'As far as being manager goes, he was an exceptional trainer but his management skills were not as good as his training skills. You have to be a good bit more subtle in management. It's a step up and there is more psychology in it and that wasn't Bobby.'

Jeff Radcliffe also remembers the 'hard man' image and adds: *'I remember Bobby and Andy Davidson used to sit in the referee's room and discuss how many legs they had broken between them, things like that. They were two of a kind.*

'The other thing about Bobby that I didn't like was that in those days on the way back from matches we used to stop for a meal. I'd be sat with Bondy from the Mail, *the bus driver, and we would sit together with Bobby and the coaching staff and he'd go round asking us all what we thought of the game and how the players did. He spoke loudly and the players were sat at the next table and could hear what we were saying. I was the physio, not the coach and felt uncomfortable giving an opinion.'*

Another with reservations about the new boss was John Hawley who never took to the new man in the manager's seat:

'Bobby and I didn't see eye to eye, it was just a personality clash but he wasn't greatly liked in the dressing room. The funny thing at that time was that the chairman was Bob Chapman and I'd known Bob for a long time because I'd gone to school with his son.

LOOK BACK IN AMBER

So he used to come into the dressing room and all the players used to have a great laugh because I used to talk to Bob as I would anybody else. Bobby Collins used to say '"Good afternoon Mr Chairman" and Bob would go "Now then John, you all right?" "Fine thanks Bob, how are you?!" So it was a big joke in the dressing room and I don't think Bobby Collins liked it.'

Whatever his failings, he was convincing the supporters and when his team beat Cardiff 4-1 shortly after his appointment as permanent manager, it looked like yet another fourteenth place was ours for the asking. Yet the Cardiff win proved to be the highpoint of Collins' rein. His decision to publicly criticise his players after the win appeared to backfire as the next nine league games brought six defeats and three draws to plunge the team into an unexpected relegation battle. City didn't record another win until January 14, by which time they had slumped into the bottom three.

Billy Bremner was still in the City midfield and the talk on Bunkers was that the job could soon be his as pressure on Collins grew. In many ways, it seemed that Collins was a short-term appointment, a suspicion reinforced by the fact that he did not write any programme notes until what turned out to be his final match, a draw with Brighton.

By this time, Collins had opted to bring in Syd Owen, also from Leeds United, as his number two but this did not appear to have any positive impact on the club which was losing pace with fellow strugglers.

City struggled in the cups too, losing to First Division Leicester in the FA Cup and reaching the fourth round of the League Cup before receiving a 5-1 thrashing at the hands of Arsenal at Highbury.

Bruce Bannister remembers a curious episode from that game: *'We went to Arsenal, getting beat 5-0 and we get a penalty. I took the penalties at that time, but John Hawley picked the ball up and told me that he was taking the penalty. I said to him get off the fucking ball, we were literally having an argument over the ball and we were 5-0 down! So I said well take it then, it didn't matter because it was only a consolation goal. I just thought if it was a goal to make it one-all, would he have taken it then?*

SLIDE DOWN THE LEAGUES

'It was out of character for John because he was as nice a lad as you could wish to meet. He had good skills for a big lad, but he was like an amateur and maybe didn't appear to have the same hunger for the job as some others.'

The team's fortunes did not improve and with relegation more of a threat the directors chose to act, though not initially with Collins losing his job. In a mysterious move, City appointed Mac Stone, the club secretary, as general manager working alongside Collins. Bob Chapman, who had taken over as chairman from Christopher Needler, said that it did not undermine the authority of Collins and was designed to help him give his full attention to the team in order to get the club out of the relegation zone.

Meanwhile, four players were transfer-listed with Malcolm Lord, City's longest-serving player, made available along with Chris Galvin, Dave Sunley and Bruce Bannister. City had agreed a fee of £15,000 with Portsmouth for Sunley but the player refused, saying he wanted to stay in the North. In other transfer activity, City were considering making a move for winger Alan Groves from Blackpool and Collins brought in Alan Hoult on loan from Leicester City while Vince Grimes was sold to Scunthorpe.

However, before these changes had chance to work and the day before City were due to travel to Stoke for a fixture, which in the event was cancelled due to poor weather, Collins was sacked, becoming City's shortest-reigning manager in history. Even though he had been in charge for just four and a half months and Syd Owen, his deputy, had been at City for just two months, City had won only one of the last 14 league and cup games and the decline had been marked.

Bob Chapman said: *'We have had a disastrous run of results. We have not had an away win under Collins's management. We are down near the bottom of the table and we had to do something drastic.'*

Ken Houghton took over in temporary charge and made his mark immediately by bringing back former playing colleague Chris Chilton to take over his old position as youth coach. He also fined six players who had turned up late for training and said, *'I want the players to be disciplined, they know the score if they step out of line. I'll be fair to them but they have to understand that I'm not going to be a soft touch.'*

Ken said: *'I got thrown in at the deep end. I was quite happy looking after the kids and reserves and bringing players forward and then suddenly I was thrust into the firing line. I wanted to be manager at some point but not at that time, it happened too quickly. I think you need some apprenticeship. Cliff Britton was my mentor and if I could have sat with him and learned off him I could have been a good manager but I suddenly went from player, brief time in charge of the youngsters and then taking over a team that is struggling. Also, when you get a team that's on the slide it's difficult to turn it round.'*

John Hawley remembered him well from his playing days at the club, just a few years previously and said:

'Ken Houghton was a great character, one of the great characters of the game. When I first came into the side, he and Ken Knighton were the two big pranksters in the club and used to play fantastic tricks on away trips to keep the morale up. His fault as a manager was probably that he was too nice.'

Bruce Bannister was another who had respect for Houghton: *'Ken was a nice fellow, but results dictate whether he was a good manager or not. At the time I don't think it was a bad team. The team which had got to fourth early on in the season under John Kaye didn't suddenly become a bad one. It just didn't happen, and I'm not blaming Ken for that because I don't think he was a poor manager but good managers get results. Possibly he was too nice to be really successful although he had Andy Davidson with him and he was someone who could be ruthless.*

'I still think throughout that time that Billy Bremner hung over it, almost like "the king is dead long live the king", but in this case the king was still stood there! Billy was obviously going to be retiring soon, a monumental figure in the game whichever way you look at it, and he was logically going to go into management in some form at some stage, yet City couldn't get Billy to make the logical step.' There was much work for Houghton to do as he embarked on his first job in management. The players appeared to be performing just when the mood took them and it was no way to turn around the fortunes of a club staring relegation in the face.

SLIDE DOWN THE LEAGUES

Despite the change in management, relegation was always a strong possibility. Since the victory over Cardiff in November under Bobby Collins, City won only three more matches all season and the drop was confirmed at Brisbane Road, home of Orient as part of a five-game losing streak which ended the season. Houghton had not succeeded in turning the club's fortunes around and the question that remained unanswered was whether, if John Kaye had still been manager, City would have gone down. The club may have stagnated during the last few months of his reign but at the end of the 1977-78 season, 14th place in Division Two would have been preferable to 22nd.

Therefore, with the side relegated, it was a busy close season for the Tigers with the new manager wanting to mould a team capable of bouncing back, hopefully towards instant promotion. City gave free transfers to team captain Billy Bremner, who was intending to retire, Dave Gibson, who had failed to live up to his early promise, and Dave Sunley and Gary Brattan, who had never made a first team appearance. The club were also willing to listen to offers for Jeff Wealands, Chris Galvin and Bruce Bannister. Wealands had lost his place to Eddie Blackburn and wanted regular first team football, Galvin had also lost his place as the team lost their way throughout the relegation season and Bruce Bannister had only managed to score four goals since his move the previous summer.

Meanwhile, Malcolm Lord, who had been listed by Bobby Collins, would have his position decided when he came back from a summer playing football for California Surfs. Another likely departure was that of Dave Roberts who was placed on the transfer list at his own request, as he wanted to play at a higher grade of football.

Peter Daniel, who had broken into the England Under-21 team had been attracting scouts to Boothferry Park all season with Leeds and West Brom among the front-runners in the chase for his signature. At one stage it appeared that Daniel would have gone to Leeds with David McNiven coming the other way but that came to nothing. Towards the end of the season Leeds came back in for Daniel and offered £60,000 plus Paul Reaney and Peter Lorimer, but a few days later he was finally sold, not to Leeds but Wolves for a fee in the region of £200,000.

Dave Roberts also got his wish for a move, securing a deal with Cardiff City for £70,000, and John Hawley went to Leeds United for a fee of about £85,000.

Hawley said: '*I didn't particularly look to leave although you always want to better yourself if you can. I always wanted to try and play at the highest level and there was a lot of talk of me moving to the First Division which was flattering and of great interest. Leeds had been trying to buy me for quite a while. It was them and Arsenal who were interested.*'

Season 1978-79

Ken Houghton had a thankless task taking over as manager when City were already in deep relegation trouble in 1977-78. However, with his first full season as manager ahead expectations were high and he brought in three new signings to replace those who had left the club. Winger John Farley came from Wolves, Micky Horswill, who won the FA Cup with Sunderland, came from Plymouth and, quite a coup, Keith Edwards was bought from Sheffield United for £60,000.

Ken Houghton said: '*You go and watch games all over the country as manager and you get players recommended to you so someone mentioned Keith Edwards. I would have liked him because he was a good goalscorer but I wondered who had the money to buy him.*

'*Jimmy Syrill was his manager and I spoke to him and asked about Edwards. He said, "You can have him. He'll get you goals but he won't do anything else." I met Keith and his wife in Doncaster and convinced him that his future was here. He was brilliant but he used to pull my hair out! I remember one game, I took him off and he went to see the chairman the next day and I got a right bollocking. I knew then that the writing was on the wall.*'

Houghton also refreshed the coaching set-up, bringing in Wilf McGuinness who had been at Manchester United. His arrival brought

SLIDE DOWN THE LEAGUES

two funny men together in the opinion of Jeff Radcliffe: '*Ken was maybe too nice to be a manager but his spell was one of the funniest, especially when he appointed Wilf McGuinness. It was great on Mondays, playing the kids in the gym with Houghie, Andy, myself and Chris Chilton. I remember Wilf chinning me once. We were both on the same side and were big pals but we were having a go at each other about something and he smacked me in the mouth, but it was all forgotten afterwards!*'

Ken Houghton recalls McGuinness: '*When I got the manager's job, one of the directors said that Matt Busby was on the phone. He recommended Wilf McGuinness for the assistant job. Now when Matt Busby talks, you listen. So I met him and he was a lovely fellow but before games he was more content to do his ball juggling for the crowd!*'

The Tigers got the new season off to a good start as Keith Edwards showed why many at Bramall Lane were sorry to see him go. He scored a hat-trick in a 3-0 win over Chester in one of the early games and City went to the top of the table in September with high hopes of an early return to the Second Division. For Bannister though, Houghton's team selection may have been a factor in the later slide down the table: '*It was a bit strange because we had big Alan here* (Warboys). *Then Keith Edwards got brought in and it was a problem in many ways because Alan didn't have anywhere to play. They didn't find a suitable role for him and that was a shame because he was still a talented player.*'

However, Warboys was still getting a place in the starting line-up with Edwards and Bannister as the two upfront. A brilliant display at home to Walsall picked out Edwards as a City hero in the making. He scored twice with Lord and Bannister also getting goals but it was Edwards' first goal which excited Boothferry Park.

Malcolm Lord cleared the ball out of the Tigers' penalty area and Edwards gained possession of the ball inside the City half. Showing great ball control and speed, he went past the defence, dribbling the ball past the last couple of defenders, drawing in the Walsall keeper and coolly slotting it past him for one of the best goals seen at City for many years.

LOOK BACK IN AMBER

Bruce Bannister remembers Keith Edwards fondly: '*I sometimes used to travel in with Keith as well and he was a very quiet boy. However, at that level, going forward, he was the best finisher I ever played with. He wasn't a good pro in terms of doing the professional things on the pitch though. Keith would never defend from the front, doing the kind of things that the spectators never see. He used to drive everyone potty as it was a team event. As soon as you lose the ball you get goalside, then you can relax a bit but not Keith! He never got back. As it happened I worked him better than anyone else as I kept him in line and because we were mates he'd listen to me.*

'*I used to train with him and there'd be targets on the goals which he used to hit every time. So he had some fantastic qualities but the reason he didn't make it at the top was the lack of work off the ball. He was interesting to work with because it was either black or white with him. He had games where he was brilliant or others where it was, "Is Keith about?"*'

City had started the new season well but a disappointing home draw with Chesterfield was followed by three successive defeats and City slid down the table.

It was a surprise to the fans and the manager. Houghton explains: '*I honestly believed at the time that we had enough to go back up. I thought we had the resources, the players to do it. I probably blame myself in a way because I thought we were good enough. At the time we were getting results and I was thinking that management was bloody easy! But it isn't like that and you can't rest on your laurels when you beat somebody. We had a really good start but then went about seven or eight games without a win and that's when directors start to talk to people when they go out on Saturday night and that's what happens.*'

In fact City only managed one more win in the next two months, though it was a high-profile one. Watford led the division and famous chairman Elton John was on *Swap Shop* on the Saturday morning explaining that he was taking a helicopter up to Hull for the game at Boothferry Park.

So Elton rode up north in a helicopter, landing at the Crest Motel in North Ferriby where he joined the players and officials of Watford who had stayed there overnight. He probably expected a win as City were in an appalling run of form but City caused a shock, winning 4-0 with Bannister scoring twice.

However, the win did not give the Tigers a kick-start to their season and poor away form especially was to put paid to any chance City had of getting anywhere near the promotion pack. With a mid-table season in the offing, there was to be no respite in the FA Cup. After making hard work of non-league Stafford Rangers in the first round, City were beaten at Carlisle in round two, though the squad had been hit by a flu virus.

In early March City went on a run of four successive defeats, sending the club towards the relegation zone, and Houghton's position was the subject of some scrutiny. It was widely believed that he was given a warning that results had to improve but whatever was said, it worked, and a run of 23 points from 15 games, scoring 23 goals and conceding only 12 between March and the end of the season, probably kept Ken Houghton in a job and quelled the mounting disquiet on the terraces.

The rest of the season was notable for some of the young players, who had been playing regularly for the reserves making their first team debuts. Houghton put great faith in a successful youth policy and it was starting to bear fruition with several ready for a first team call-up. Pete Skipper, playing at left-back, was first, later to be joined by Garreth Roberts and Craig Norrie.

Ken remembers: '*I was youth team manager and so worked with Steve McClaren, Garreth Roberts, Brian Marwood, Gary Swann and others before they made the first team. I always knew that Garreth would make it. Garreth was the one that you could put into any side and you wouldn't have to tell him what to do, if he'd been six foot he'd have been in the England side. When a player is making his first team debut and I'm telling other players what to do in the game and I don't have to tell him, that tells you all you need to know about Garreth.*

'*Brian was different. He was a lovely lad and still is but if he didn't play to his best, his head used to go down and we had to lift him. I couldn't have a go at him the way I did with some others, I always used to have to lift him up. I remember going up to Sunderland to meet him and his parents to sign him on. They said to me, "Look after him" and I did because that was my job.*'

LOOK BACK IN AMBER

It was a special time for Garreth Roberts, making his debut for his home-town club: *"I'd been a fan of City since I was at school. I lived in Willerby and my mum and dad used to go and watch in the Wagstaff and Chilton era and I've been a fan ever since. They got us a season ticket in the Best Stand and it was the era when everybody used to sit in the same seat for years and it was great.*

'I was lucky that Ken Houghton was my first youth team boss. I remembered him as a player and respected what he had done. When Houghie got the job as first team manager, I got Chillo, so I went from Houghton to Chilton and I couldn't get much better than that.

'The junior side I was in won the Northern Intermediate League for the first time ever including players such as Rob McDonald, Craig Norrie, Dave Hawker and Willie Boyd, and I had a few games in the reserves before I made my first team debut. The main reason I got into the team at that time was because the first team weren't doing that well so he threw in three or four of the kids, myself, Brian Marwood and Pete Skipper.

'The dressing room for the first time was a daunting place because there was a lot of banter and as a kid I was awestruck although I had been an apprentice. I was bootboy and kitboy so I was involved with the first team in some respects, but I must have kept my mouth shut for about a year!'

The season ended with a 3-2 win over Sheffield Wednesday and, with a final position of eighth, the season had ended positively with promotion a realistic ambition for the following year. Bob Chapman therefore renewed Houghton's job for the 1979-80 season.

With several youngsters pushing at the first team door, Houghton tried to move some of the more established players aside. Jeff Wealands was put on offer along with Stuart Croft who had not quite fulfilled the promise he had shown when he broke into the side during the mid 1970s, forming a good defensive partnership with Dave Roberts. Roger DeVries was also made available but was perhaps not so saleable, as he was a one-club man who was thought reluctant to want to move on at this stage of his career.

SLIDE DOWN THE LEAGUES

Alan Warboys was also put on offer and Chris Galvin left the club, joining Stockport County. Meanwhile, Dave Stewart was released; a sad end to a City career for the Northern Ireland winger who had made such an impression when he first broke into the team at the start of the 1976-77, though since then he had not been consistent enough or determined enough to figure as a regular first team player.

Season 1979-80

The beginning of the 1979-80 season saw a new City team with Jeff Wealands, Alan Warboys, Chris Galvin and Dave Stewart, all major figures during City's time in the Second Division, having left the club and the one major addition to the squad being Trevor Phillips who was signed from Rotherham for £75,000, a club record.

City lost the first game at home to Colchester but then went seven games unbeaten and in October, City were handily placed in sixth with much of the credit for the change in fortune coming from a midfield which had been strengthened by Houghton bringing in Mick Tait from Carlisle for £150,000, overtaking Phillips as City's record signing, and Paul Moss who came from Wolves for £47,500 after an impressive loan spell.

To many, the partnership between Edwards and Bannister had worked well, but Houghton was determined to bring in another forward. He said: '*I look back on signing Trevor Phillips and I think "Why?!" He was playing with a big centre forward and I wondered if he could play alongside Keith Edwards. I thought he could, but he couldn't. They were too similar as players but at the time I thought it would work out. However, on that one I have to hold my hands up and say it didn't.*

'*I didn't really think that Bruce and Keith were that compatible and as Bruce was coming towards the end of his career anyway, that's why Trevor Phillips was brought in. I didn't think that a big target man was definitely the answer as I preferred playing balls to feet and players feeding off that.*'

LOOK BACK IN AMBER

After the encouraging early season form, City then went on a 15-game run without a win stretching from October through to January, their worst spell for 44 years, which plunged the club into the heart of a relegation battle. City also went out of the FA Cup, succumbing to Carlisle after a replay at Boothferry Park.

Houghton remembers: '*The cup game against Carlisle was a game we had to win. We drew at their place but they beat us at Boothferry Park and for the first time the crowd turned against me with "Houghton out".*'

By December 1979 City had not won any of the last 10 games and were facing heavy financial losses. The club had a wage bill of about £5,000 a week but only £1,800 was taken at the gate for the game against Wimbledon with a crowd of 3,750, the lowest of the season. As the Tigers were too close for comfort down near the bottom of the table, there was little likelihood of the gates increasing in the near future.

Bob Chapman said that the club could not run on gates of that size, especially as they had spent almost £300,000 on players and the club held a board meeting on the Tuesday following the Wimbledon game with speculation growing on Houghton's position, especially with the chairman pointedly refusing to back his manager.

After the meeting, the directors issued a stark warning to Houghton to get results and also to start pruning his playing staff. The manager attended the meeting and said that he felt there was not a lot wrong with the club but that everyone had to battle hard for success.

City's next game was going to be crucial as fans waited to see whether the players would try and play for their manager's future. Sadly the side were thrashed 7-2 at Brentford, one of the heaviest defeats in the club's history and a humiliation to those supporters who went down to Griffin Park. It was City's eleventh game without a win and any hopes Houghton had of keeping his job were surely laid to rest.

The following Wednesday, to nobody's surprise, City sacked Ken Houghton, also disposing of coach Wilf McGuinness and more surprisingly chief scout Andy Davidson, who had been at the club since 1948.

SLIDE DOWN THE LEAGUES

Ken Houghton said: '*ITV were doing a programme on Grimsby, Scunthorpe and City so Martin Tyler was at the ground. I said to him, "Martin, I think I might have a better story for you" because the directors were at the ground and I thought I was going to get the sack. We'd been beaten 7-2 at Brentford and I always look back at that game and think we could have been five up ourselves at half-time. They scored six headers from corners and I wouldn't have backed anyone to do that against Croftie and Dobbo because they were good in the air, it was just one of those games at a time when we needed to win.*

'*They got Andy Davidson and Wilf McGuinness in first and told them they were sacked and not to come to the club again and then asked me to resign. I refused and they said they either had to sack me or get me to resign, so I said they had better sack me. However, unlike Andy and Wilf, they said I was welcome back at the club any time I wanted.*'

Houghton remains a popular figure with Tigers fans today and, though few were surprised to see him go, his goodwill lasted, largely because he had become such a fan of City and appeared to genuinely love the club, a fact demonstrated when he sat in the stands watching City lose at home to Blackburn in the first game following his departure from Boothferry Park.

On his sacking he said that a manager's performance was governed by results and he added, '*I'm upset that Wilf and Andy have been given the sack. I was the manager and it should have been just my job that was on the line, but it's a sad day. I love Hull City.*'

Houghton adds: '*I stayed at Boothferry Park for another couple of hours, clearing my desk, and it really hit me. I cried when I left because I would have loved to have followed it through and made a success of it. I went to the next home game, we lost at home to Blackburn and the support I got was incredible.*'

Garreth Roberts, grateful to the man who made him captain of his hometown club, remembers him with affection: '*He was the manager who gave me my first team opportunity so he's God as far as I'm concerned. He gave me and others our opportunity and he had the guts to do that and he also tried to wheedle out those who he may have thought were the bad apples that were in there. He put the club on a good standing for future years but he didn't get the chance to carry it out, which was a shame. Houghie was one of the first ones to bring the kids through and that team was to set the scene for the promotion seasons we had.*

'The perception with Ken Houghton was that he was too easy or too soft. He's a really top man so perhaps that was a valid point but it all comes down to results. If it doesn't work out on the pitch you can be nice or hard, it doesn't matter. With Houghie, if he did shout you used to think it was a bit forced. He was very passionate about the game but he's quite well spoken, so it didn't really work.'

Immediately after Houghton's departure, the news buzzing around the football world was that the manager of the Welsh national team, Mike Smith, was the man that Chapman wanted to become City's new manager. City were said to have already approached the Welsh FA with a view to talking to Smith and within days the rumours were confirmed and Mike Smith and his assistant, Bobby Brown, were released from their duties to take over at City, though they would not officially start at Boothferry Park until 1 January 1980.

Smith had tendered his resignation which the Welsh FA accepted 'with regret' and City agreed compensation, paying up the remaining seven months of Smith and Brown's contracts. The Welsh FA said; *'There was no point in making a last minute attempt to keep him because we simply could not match Hull's offer. Our finances would not allow it.'* Smith also recruited Cyril Lea from Ipswich Town as part of his management team.

Smith was to come to Hull with a formidable reputation, having led Wales to the European Championship quarter-finals during his five and a half years in charge and, after securing Smith's signature, Chapman called it, *'a historic day for the club'.* He added: *'It has been our ambition to achieve First Division status, which has always eluded us, and with the new management team we are confident we have the right set-up for the next decade.'*

The news that Smith was to take over did not improve City's fortunes on the pitch as, following the Blackburn defeat, they were now without a win in 11 games, the longest run without a victory in

SLIDE DOWN THE LEAGUES

28 years. Unusually the team for the next game, away at Oxford over the Christmas period, was picked by Bob Chapman himself along with director Ian Blakey and Chris Chilton, but it too ended in defeat and the Tigers badly needed the impetus a new manager often brings.

So Smith and his team arrived on January 1 1980 and the board also had plans off the field to improve the club. At the turn of the year, before Smith took up his role at Boothferry Park, Chairman Bob Chapman had announced plans for a huge, fully-integrated sports and shopping complex, estimated to cost £1.5m, which had been given the go-ahead at the planning stage. The three-storey complex would feature a Jackson's supermarket together with a warehouse and a ticket office on the ground floor. The second floor would be a sports centre along with offices for the football club and the top floor would be an 800 square metre clubroom. City hoped that the plan would become reality by about 1982.

On the field, the new manager was soon ringing the changes. In came Nick Deacy, a Welsh international who had played for, amongst others, PSV Eindhoven and Vitesse Arnhem. Also coming in were Burnley keeper Tony Norman and Ipswich central defender Dale Roberts.

However, there were lots of players going the other way. Ian Dobson and Paul Moss were made available for offer, Malcolm Lord retired, Derek Hood moved to York and Willie Boyd moved to Doncaster. Further departures in March saw Dave Hawker join Darlington and Trevor Phillips leave for Chester, with Eddie Blackburn transferred to York.

It was a time of great change at Boothferry Park and none of the playing staff felt safe in the team with players arriving and departing with great regularity. Bruce Bannister played relatively few games for the new management team and said: '*I was fortunate with injuries throughout my career but unusually I was struck down with a virus when Mike Smith came from the Welsh job and Cyril Lea followed him from Ipswich. At the time I was 11 stone and I lost about 10 pounds which was a lot when you are a fit athlete. So I was away for over a week and then had to get match-fit again and this was a time with a new management team who were making assessments about everybody. It was about a month before I was back to the physique I'd had before the illness but by that time I was back playing in the first team so it was a strain on me.'*

He also had instant doubts about the new management team: *'Smith was very stand-offish. Cyril Lea used to do all the motivational stuff and most of the training. Again, he didn't do well with City but he'd had some good results with Wales.'*

Despite the wholesale changes, the arrival of Mike Smith did bring about an improvement in performances at home with eight wins from eleven games, though the team's away form was just as appalling with just three points out of a possible 20.

Edwards' goals continued to give the Tigers some respite but City were nevertheless in danger of going down to the Fourth Division for the first time in the club's history with much depending on the penultimate game of the season, at home to Southend United who were also struggling at the bottom.

Only 3,200 were at Boothferry Park for such an important game, mainly because, according to the media, most of the population had left Hull behind to spend the day in London with Hull FC and Hull Kingston Rovers meeting at Wembley in the final of the Rugby League Challenge Cup. Much was made of the contrast in fortunes between the football and rugby sides but City at least restored some credibility to the major sport as the few remaining in Hull saw Keith Edwards score the goal that gave City the points needed to save themselves from the drop.

The players waved to the fans from the directors' box afterwards in a show of appreciation but the fact that they were celebrating not going down to the Fourth Division served merely to show how far the club had fallen in the last three or four years.

Though City were safe, they finished only one place above the drop zone and the Mike Smith revolution had not yet worked its magic, despite a huge turnaround in the playing staff. Jeff Radcliffe had his doubts about the new management team's training methods:

'Mike Smith was a great organiser. He took everyone to Carnegie in Leeds to have their fitness assessed by a sports scientist so they were put on treadmills with ECGs on them and oxygen bags to analyse the gas they were breathing out. They got their results back and it came out that people like Garreth and

SLIDE DOWN THE LEAGUES

Steve McClaren had fitness levels no better than the average man in the street and they were two of the squad who could run forever!

'The Carnegie people designed a fitness regime for the players which involved them running five days a week round the track at Boothferry Park, doing anything from 50 yards to four laps at a time. They were doing this on a Friday as well, which is usually a day for footballers to try and conserve energy. So when it came round to Saturday, they were shattered. There was a groove right round the perimeter of the pitch where they had been running.

'I felt sorry for them, you'd see them there on a morning in the dressing room and usually there was a lot of banter, but they were so quiet and when you've got a dressing room like that, forget it.'

The end of the season saw Ian Bennyworth and Steve McClaren make their debuts and, as with Ken Houghton, it was a youthful side turning out if not, at that time, a successful one.

However, the relief in avoiding relegation did not disguise the fact that 1979-80 was City's worst ever season in terms of league placing. The club finished in 64th place in the Football League, 20th in Division Three, only escaping relegation by a single point.

There were few positives to come out of the campaign though Keith Edwards did as well as ever in attack whilst in defence Stuart Croft and Gordon Nisbet were consistent. Midfield was the key area that needed strengthening before the 1980-81 season got underway as City too often lacked midfield control with Tait and Moss not producing the performances they showed they were capable of.

At the end of the season, in a bid to reduce the wage bill further, John Farley, Bruce Bannister and Roger DeVries were released and Peter Skipper was loaned to Scunthorpe before signing permanently for Darlington. The one unplanned departure was that of Mick Tait who had earlier asked for a transfer, though he stayed until the end of the campaign.

Bruce Bannister's time at the club could not be said to have been successful and he left City with some regrets. He said: *'I enjoyed my football at Hull though it was a frustrating time. It went downhill from John leaving and continued going downhill after I'd left. It seemed to be right when I first started at the club but then John left and it just went backwards. I liked Hull and the people though they were different to West Yorkshire folk! It was just a shame that we didn't have any success there.'*

Season 1980-81

Mike Smith had nearly taken us down but as the 1980-81 season got underway he still broadly had the support of the fans. His new goalkeeper Tony Norman looked like a good buy and, with such a pedigree, fans were hoping that Nick Deacy would take the division by storm this season after a disappointing start to his Hull City career.

In addition the commercial side of the club was taking off under the guidance of Gordon Dimbleby, the club's commercial manager. We had a great new kit made by Adidas, a statement of intent in itself at the time, and a professionally-produced programme. It may have been mostly made up of a nationwide supplement which had little or no interest to City fans, but the rest of the programme was excellent, winning the Third Division 'Programme of the Season'.

Dimbleby's comments in the programme, meanwhile, were an invitation to City fans to suspend reality for a little while as despite the team's performances in the Third Division, if you read his comments you could have been forgiven for thinking that we were aiming for Liverpool to slip up at the top of the First Division for us to take our rightful place.

The 1980-81 season began with pre-season friendlies under the guise of the Anglo-Scottish Cup, a curious tournament which would perhaps have gripped the imagination a little more if we had actually played any Scottish teams. I don't remember us facing anyone other than Lincoln, Sheffield United and Grimsby.

The season itself started badly and it was not until our eighth league game, at home to Portsmouth, that we got our first win. However, it didn't kickstart our season which got steadily worse and we didn't win again until November, by which time we had lost seven league games in a row and were firmly rooted to the bottom of the table, despite the goals of Keith Edwards.

Of equal concern to supporters was the sale of key players. Paul Haigh went to Carlisle United for £100,000 and though he hadn't developed as we might have hoped when he made an England Under-21 appearance, he was nevertheless a quality player who, we hoped, would stay with the club as it tried to move its way back up the leagues.

Another unpopular move with the supporters saw Gordon Nisbet sold to Plymouth Argyle for just £30,000 whilst yet another long serving player, who had been with the club since the Second Division days, Stuart Croft, joined Portsmouth. These were important departures and there were concerns about the calibre of some of the players coming in at this time to replace them. The likes of Billy Whitehurst, Brian Ferguson, Steve Hoolikin and Stuart Eccleston appeared to be worse than the players leaving.

Some salvation in the season came once again in the FA Cup. City beat Halifax Town 2-1 with a couple of goals from Keith Edwards before being drawn to play non-league Blyth Spartans, again at Boothferry Park. The teams drew at Boothferry with Edwards scoring for City and one Les Mutrie replying for Blyth. In the replay Blyth took the lead before Edwards scored a late equaliser and the teams were due to replay the game again, this time at neutral Elland Road.

A great memory of that second replay was the 'football special' train which took us from Hull to Leeds and the thousands of City fans taking over the Leeds Kop. In a memorable game City reached the Third Round due to goals from Norrie and Stuart Croft (before his transfer) with that man Les Mutrie scoring again for Blyth. With great foresight, Mike Smith immediately snapped up Mutrie after the tie, recognising that he was capable of making an impact in the Football League.

We beat Doncaster 1-0 at home in round three before being drawn away to Tottenham in the Fourth Round. Thousands of City fans made the trip down south to support the team against the likes of Hoddle and Ardiles and those in a crowded terrace had to face a barrage of abuse and various objects thrown from the seats above us where Spurs fans were sat. City raised their game for the tie and, with Tony Norman performing heroics in goal, made it to within seven minutes of what would have been a deserved replay before Brook and Archibald gave Spurs victory. However, the fans gave City a great ovation and were proud of the team in what was a brief highlight in a ghastly season for the Tigers.

The cup run did not improve fortunes in the league with the team never looking likely to move off the bottom of the table. Keith Edwards, inevitably the leading scorer with 13 in the league, threw his shirt in disgust at Mike Smith in the dugout after being substituted in a goalless draw with Brentford in February 1981 and asked for a transfer shortly afterwards, saying that he didn't want to play in the Fourth Division.

For the players, the endless runs and the schoolmasterly tone of the manager began to grate as results on the field showed no signs of improving. Garreth Roberts said: '*Mike Smith was a nice bloke but he was really teacher-pupil sort of orientated. I remember him coming up with lines about things like the POMO line. The POMO Line is a position of maximum opportunity, but to me and you it's the far post! He came up with things like that which if results go for you, everyone sees you as a genius. We used to go down to Malham Avenue for training and I remember training in seven inches of snow and doing ten 200 metres runs and things like that. Results didn't go for us and the dressing room suffered a bit.*'

The club was still being run professionally off the pitch but there were noticeable cracks appearing in the façade and relations between the club and supporters were entering a new low. The truly depressing season had become too much for some fans who launched the Action Group and towards the end of the season, with City condemned to relegation to the Fourth Division, there were coffins being led down Boothferry Road and 'flags of surrender' at the Swindon Town game.

The Action Group aimed to get involved in City's problems on and off the field and came up with a proposal to ask Raich Carter to return to the club as General Manager in an attempt to improve City's poor position in the league. It didn't happen but there was the feeling that change would have to be brought about by the supporters if it was not forthcoming in the boardroom.

Even the worryingly optimistic Gordon Dimbleby had to refer to the fact that the club was not in an ideal position to push on for that European place we'd been eyeing. He mentioned that he would be meeting some of the demonstrators and added, *'Fellow Tigers, I'm your man and so when we do get together let your thoughts and ideas be for the future well-being of Hull City AFC.'*

The few bright points in the league season came towards the end when the team was already down. The next home game after the infamous Swindon game was against Huddersfield and City won the derby 2-1 with a goal from Nick Deacy just a minute from the end of the game. The penultimate home game of the season was against Sheffield United and with City already down, it was of little interest to us, though Sheffield were involved in a struggle to avoid being relegated alongside the Tigers.

Deacy scored again, this time after only four minutes which triggered a pitch invasion by the Sheffield supporters. They equalised and headed for home confident they would escape the drop but thankfully they didn't as they lost at home to Wrexham in the last game to claim the last relegation place, though a few seasons later the Blades would get their revenge on us.

Only 2,059 fans saw the last game of the season, a 3-1 win over Newport County as the club prepared for life in the Fourth Division for the first time in their history.

Season 1981-82

Season 1981-82 saw City in the Fourth Division for the first time in the club's history and a youthful squad, including the likes of Norman, Garreth, Dale and John Roberts, Marwood, McClaren and a very raw Billy Whitehurst, embarked on the new season. Keith Edwards was still at Boothferry, though unsettled and on offer for £150,000. However, with Edwards and Les Mutrie upfront, the team did at least look like scoring goals. Losing away to Torquay on the first day, City recovered by beating Bradford at Boothferry Park in the first Yorkshire derby of the season, and the next home game saw another as Sheffield United came to Hull and over 7,000 saw City beat the Blades courtesy of a late goal from Keith Edwards in front of Bunkers.

Maybe it was the fact that the goal was against his old club but Edwards seemed distinctly cool about scoring, and suspicions turned to fact when he was immediately sold back to our South Yorkshire rivals. Even worse was the news that we only received £75,000 for a striker who had shown himself capable of scoring regularly even in the worse teams. In hindsight, his departure for that fee showed that the club were in a deeper mess financially than most fans had feared. The loss of Edwards meant a vacancy upfront, which was filled by Billy Whitehurst, probably a year too early.

Despite Edwards' departure, City did have Les Mutrie upfront and were still scoring. The problems were in defence where they conceded 24 goals in ten games despite playing five men at the back. However, once the formation of Nick Deacy, Dale Roberts and Gary Swann were brought into the centre of the defence, with Swann playing as sweeper, the slide was stopped and the team put together a nine-game unbeaten sequence.

Though City's form was poor in the lead up to Christmas, the team were doing well again in the FA Cup, beating Rochdale, though we were forced into a second replay at Elland Road for the second year in a row, and then beating Hartlepool 2-0 at Boothferry Park. The reward was an away tie at Chelsea who were still a good draw despite being in the Second Division.

The original game was called off due to a frozen pitch but in the rearranged game City played well at Stamford Bridge on a freezing cold Monday night to keep the score at 0-0 and force a replay back at Boothferry Park. A crowd of 13,238 saw Chelsea win the game 2-0 but the game was remembered chiefly for violence near to the ground with running battles on Boothferry Road and near the South Stand entrance on North Road. Someone also threw a bottle through the Chelsea coach window whilst the team were driving back down south on the A63, some of the glass hitting goalkeeper Steve Francis who was lucky not to have been blinded.

SLIDE DOWN THE LEAGUES

The relative success in the cup did not bring the crowds flocking back to Boothferry Park; even the first home game of the season, the local derby against Bradford, only brought in 3,900 and by the time of the home game with Hartlepool in February, a month after the Chelsea game, gates were down to below 3,000 with the effect on the finances becoming critical. The Hartlepool game itself was a success with City winning 5-2, Les Mutrie scoring four of them, but problems off the field were coming to a head. City were losing £9,000 a week, mostly as a result of the wage bill, headed by the large salaries collected by Mike Smith, Cyril Lea, Bobby Brown and Gordon Dimbleby. City had banked on the manager taking the club back up to the Second Division but the strategy had failed and the club was struggling in the Fourth and not looking likely to get back to the Third at the first time of asking.

Just five days after the Hartlepool game, on February 25th 1982, the club became the first in the country to call in the official receiver with Christopher Needler taking finance company Branwick's advice to stop funding the club.

Being the first club to suffer this fate left supporters confused; was the club up for sale, was it going to be relegated, closed down, what? The official receiver, Martin Spencer, placed the entire playing staff on the transfer list and said that the 'Boothferry Seven' who were the highest-paid players at the club, namely John Davies, Dennis Booth, Nick Deacy, Brian Ferguson, Dale Roberts, Micky Horswill and Billy Whitehurst, were to be given until March 15th to find other clubs or be dismissed. From almost getting a vague thrill that the news of receivership had placed City in the newspapers, the news of the impending dismissals proved to supporters how grave the situation had become.

Jeff Radcliffe says: '*I remember the players were all sat in the bath at Aldershot singing "on the dole" and there was a big picture on the front of the Mail, showing all the staff and speculating on whether we'd keep our jobs. We didn't know what was going to happen but luckily Don came in and what a character he was! The players went on a really good run whilst the club was in receivership but they were all playing for their futures knowing they could well be on their way to another club.*'

LOOK BACK IN AMBER

Garreth Roberts, the team captain at the time, added: '*The media interest was nothing like it is today. We probably had a small section on the back of the* Hull Daily Mail *because we took it in turn with the rugby clubs; whoever was doing well got more coverage. I can't remember how I first heard about the receivership but I think it was a gradual process of realising that there were problems at the club.*

'*Once we did go into receivership I remember all the meetings we used to have. Mickey Horswill was around that time and I think he may have been the union rep. He was a great lad, always on for a good night out. Gordon Taylor was coming down all the time and it was a bit scary because you didn't really know what was going on. Some of the older lads sussed it out and thought, well we'd better get out of here.*'

City played again at home the following Saturday with Mansfield being the visitors for 'What could be the last ever Hull City game', a headline that would be seen several more times in later years. At least the team was performing on the pitch with threats of dismissal possibly spurring them on. A crowd of just under 5,000, 2,000 up on the previous game, saw City win 2-0 with goals from Flounders and Mutrie.

Another home game followed on the Tuesday night and again there was a good crowd 6,952, who saw the team beat Halifax 2-0 through Mutrie (again) and Davis. By the time City played away at Darlington in late March, only a defeat at top-of-the-table Wigan had stopped City recording seven successive victories, which had moved the club away from the lower mid-table position into the top ten with promotion unlikely but still possible.

By this time, Mike Smith and Cyril Lea had been given their cards by the receiver along with Gordon Dimbleby and the team was being run by Bobby Brown and Chris Chilton, who had been spared. Crowds were creeping up towards the 5-6,000 mark as the football improved and, though still in receivership, the team was playing with style and perhaps a little freedom. Nick Deacy and Micky Horswill became the only two to leave Boothferry Park, both of them joining Happy Valley in Hong Kong, but the other members of the seven had been reprieved.

SLIDE DOWN THE LEAGUES

Garreth Roberts felt that the spirit amongst the players was key in helping the club survive:

'People weren't particularly upset to see Mike Smith leave the club but it was still a shock and we realised then that we had to pull together if we were going to make a career in the game and make sure that the results on the pitch were going our way. There were a few of the older lads who did help in the pulling together but they also had it in their minds that they had to be realistic and think about the best for their families, so if they could get out they would.

'We went on a really good run from the February onwards until the end of that season, finishing about eighth, and that set us up for the next season. Bobby Brown and Chris Chilton were caretakers in their first management appointment and the fact that they were doing it together helped them.'

City's form through to the end of the season was good and the team were still in with a faint chance of promotion after Easter, but successive draws with Crewe and Stockport put paid to those hopes and we finished a respectable eighth in the table with most hoping for a promotion challenge the season after if we could hold onto the players and someone came in to buy the club.

The back page of the *Mail* had plenty of rumours about who was interested in taking the club on but in the meantime, players wanted to know their futures and there was renewed concern when five City players, whose contracts expired at the end of July, were give free transfers by the club. The players - Tony Norman, Billy Whitehurst, Bobby McNeil, Gary Swann and Andy Flounders - were given letters to say that they were not to be offered new terms.

Norman especially was annoyed about the way the business was handled, publicly criticising the fact that the five of them were handed the letters at the club in front of other players. Norman expected to be signing for Birmingham City before the new season as he had gone there for transfer talks in March but the Midlands club pulled out when they realised that City wanted a fee for him. With no fee now expected, the way was clear for him to join them.

By May 1982, the end of the season approached and the club was still in the hands of the official receiver. There was talk of a possible bid from Hull FC with Hull chairman Roy Waudby intending to get in touch with the receiver to inform him of his interest. This move followed discussions with a consortium of Hull businessmen and members of a sub-committee at the Boulevard who had been looking into a possible ground-share at Boothferry Park. The consortium themselves had had a bid of their own rejected by Christopher Needler.

However, also in the running was Don Robinson who had already held talks with the receiver Adrian Rapazzini, who had taken over the running of the club from Martin Spencer. A day after the Halifax away game, the final game of the 1981-82 season, it was announced that the club had been saved. Hilary Needler, the widow of Harold, had set up a foundation in memory of her late husband, which had offered to buy the club and it was the higher of the two offers, the other coming from Hull FC.

The setting up of the fund by the Needler family was to ensure that Boothferry Park remained as a sports facility and effectively cleared the club's massive debts. In addition there was money to spare for compensation for the management team of Smith, Lea and Dimbleby who had been sacked in March. The deal also involved Don Robinson who acquired a significant shareholding in the company, becoming the largest shareholder and taking over as chairman of the football club.

Don Robinson had made his name at Flamingo Park where he had turned an old country house and 25 acres of ground into a country leisure park. He also transformed 50 disused tennis courts into Yorkshire's largest marine park, Scarborough Zoo and Marineland, and took over the Royal Opera House in Scarborough, making it one of only two independent theatres making a profit in the country. He arrived at Scarborough Football Club with it having debts of £150,000 and left with the club having £400,000 worth of assets. Colin Appleton, who Robinson had known from his schooldays in Scarborough, became manager of Scarborough and the two of them had turned the club into one of the country's top non-league outfits.

Robinson said: '*I'd been at Scarborough and three years out of four we'd been to Wembley and in those days clubs were lucky to break even. I started a lottery at Scarborough and we were able to build new stands, new floodlights, a new boardroom and plush dressing rooms. I was doing it for nothing, for my home town. At one time Scarborough made over a quarter of a million pounds, which is about two or three million today.*

'Out of the blue I got an approach from the administrator at Hull City, who asked if I'd be interested in the club. It wasn't far away and I had links with Hull through Kingston Rovers. Also, I like new challenges so I got involved, but again it wasn't for money, it was for the involvement in sport and wanting to win. So I went and talked, then I met up with the Needler family. I ended up buying the voting shares in the club for £1 but the Needler family had some debt and they took that out of non-voting.'

Robinson immediately made the headlines, saying that he would hand over to somebody else in a couple of years' time if he had not made the club financially viable and successful on the field. He warned that the following season would be hard because there were financial cuts to be made to get the house in order. However, most of his rhetoric was relentlessly upbeat, refreshingly so after the dark days of receivership. He said that he was a winner and only wanted other people who thought of themselves as winners to play for the club.

On his first day of business, Don Robinson worked on the process of taking the club out of receivership by picking a new board and making preliminary plans for the following season. He called the City players into his office one by one to explain to them his hopes for the campaign ahead and spelt out the need for them to take a cut in appearance money. Meanwhile, Norman, Whitehurst, McNeil, Swann and Flounders, who had originally been expected to leave the club, were now given offers to stay at Boothferry Park. Robinson also wanted to persuade both Bobby Brown and Chris Chilton to stay after guiding the team into a good position following Smith's sacking.

PART THREE

The Robinson renaissance

Season 1982-83

Don Robinson took over at Boothferry Park to be presented with a three-sided ground with an empty space where the North Stand once stood.

From the mid-Sixties onwards, Boothferry Park was in many ways a classic football ground of its time. The two ends saw large banks of terracing with seating on top, the east side of the ground was a large covered terrace and at the opposite end was the main stand or 'Best Stand' as it was referred to by locals. With the club's decline - gates had fallen by the mid to late Seventies - came the first signs that Boothferry Park was becoming past its best and by the late 1970s, as the club was facing life outside the top two divisions, came the first plans for the redevelopment of the North Stand.

Originally the plans were quite grand. Despite the club's decline, the ambitious board of directors, led by Bob Chapman, saw the scheme as a way of increasing revenue and launching the club back to promotion and a further tilt at the First Division. The plans included a superstore on the North Stand car park with another car park built on the other side of the Boothferry Halt railway line. Above the superstore would be built a huge sporting and leisure complex and a social club for supporters to replace the one which was already housed in the North Stand.

The directors quickly realised that the plan was too ambitious for the money they had available and a decision was made to demolish the original stand and build the complex in its place with executive boxes facing the pitch and seats replacing the terrace in the East Stand. It was also planned to build a tunnel under the railway to enable fans to get to the ground this way but the club became embroiled in a dispute with British Rail, though this was not the only reason for the plans being shelved.

With the club's financial problems taking root, receivership became a growing threat and the North Stand was eventually demolished with nothing in its place. Though there were plans for a supermarket, for some months Boothferry Park was a three-sided ground with wooden boards separating the pitch from the car park and Boothferry Road behind it. It was a sad end for a stand which was such a focal point for Boothferry Park. Being so far from my position at the top of the South Stand, I always used to wonder who actually went in the North; it never used to make any noise and I didn't know anyone who stood or sat there. All the same, I was glad it was there and it looked impressive topped off, of course, with the Hull Savings Bank clock. To those of us who had become used to it, Boothferry Park was never the same when the North Stand came down.

So Don Robinson was presented with a piece of land ready for development and typically his plans appealed to supporters. The *Hull Daily Mail*, ever eager to report the chairman's intentions, led with his plans for a Hollywood-style bowl facing the pitch which would attract the top music acts to the city. Neighbours objected to the threat of noise pollution despite Robinson telling them that the noise would be no worse than that given out by the PA system on a normal matchday. However, the scheme got as far as receiving planning permission in 1984 and it was hoped that building work would begin later that year.

Like one or two other Robinson plans, such as City playing on the moon, it never got off the ground but the Jackson's supermarket was built along with club offices. Facing the pitch was a small piece of open terracing which was given over to away fans, apart from one game in 1996, but more of that later!

Robinson said: '*City were the first to have a supermarket on the ground, which helped to pay off the debts, and a lot of others followed suit. We hoped to do a Hollywood Bowl and were always looking to do something with the top of the North Stand but never managed it.*'

The plans for a Hollywood Bowl were typical Robinson hype, but it was showmanship that City badly needed after the grim experience of receivership. Garreth Roberts felt that Robinson was exactly what City needed at the time: '*Don was so enthusiastic. It was his first step in the league arena but he was such a showman, such as when he rode around the edge of the pitch on horseback! Also he threw sweets to the crowd and got us to kick footballs into the crowd, dead cheap plastic footballs, but it was great. We used to go to Scarborough quite a bit because that was where he was based and I remember we went to one of the theme parks. I've got a picture somewhere of him trying to get me to put my head in a dolphin's mouth. It was daft stuff but it got us noticed. We went to hospitals, did charity work, and got noticed around town. He even took us to Florida where we played games against Tampa Bay and Fort Lauderdale.*

'Many of us might have wanted to just train and play and leave it at that but Don made you go and face Joe Public and get some respect for yourself and the club. Not many teams used to go and want to play for the chairman because they are usually so aloof, but he was different. He used to come in after games, saying 'drinks are on me' and stuff like that.

'Once we got past the receivership we had to get together, really bond and get the camaraderie going and that's what Don was good at, blending it all together. He was a top man. He did some really weird things and said some weird things but the spirit for those five, six years between 81-82 through to 87-88 was incredible.'

At the start of 1982-83, City's second season in the Fourth Division, they were in immeasurably better shape than a year earlier. The owners of a fresh balance sheet following several years of being wholly in debt, Robinson had made an instant impact at Boothferry Park. He had reduced losses by £100,000 though he kept season ticket prices at the same level, had persuaded Bobby Brown to return to the club in a part-time capacity as youth liaison officer and had the new terms to Billy Whitehurst, Bobby McNeil, Tony Norman, Gary Swann and Andy Flounders accepted so the players returned to the club in time for pre-season training.

Chris Chilton also accepted Robinson's offer to stay at Boothferry Park but the new managerial face was Colin Appleton, who had paired up so successfully with Robinson at Scarborough.

Robinson said: *'The first thing I did was bring in Colin Appleton who'd been with me at Scarborough. He was a great team-builder in a sense and that was the only way I thought the club could be brought back because we didn't have fortunes to spend, we had to make it profitable by getting the debt down.*

LOOK BACK IN AMBER

'*Chris Chilton did a lot to help. I was going to make him manager and have Colin as assistant. I rang Chris the night before I was going to call a press conference to announce the new manager but he asked me for a couple more days to think about it. So I picked Colin up the following day and told him he was going to be manager. He was shocked but agreed.*

'*To give Chris great credit, when I told him that Colin was going to be manager, I told him that if he wanted the assistant post it was his. A lot of people would have been funny but Chris wasn't and they worked together very well. Chris never seemed to bear a grudge and it was a great team partnership.*

'*I'd known Colin at Scarborough and from my schooldays and he was a dour manager but he was great with players and with Chillo having a different personality, it clicked. Chris was Hull City-mad which helped, so it worked well. My job was just to sort the finances out and the first year we broke even and made a profit every year after that, which is how it should be.*'

The new manager had virtually the same staff at his disposal as Brown and Chilton had towards the end of the previous season. Apart from Horswill and Deacy, the only other departures were Craig Norrie, who had moved to Holland to continue his career, whilst both Brian Ferguson and Stuart Eccleston were released at the end of the previous season.

Appleton made relatively few acquisitions though one popular move was in re-signing Peter Skipper, who came back home from Darlington for £10,000, a fee paid for by the fans.

Don Robinson said: '*It was a great help having Chris Chilton at the club when we arrived because he loved the club and knew what had gone on before. The first signing we made was Peter Skipper, who had been at the club and had gone to Darlington and it was Chris who said that he was a hell of a good central defender and we needed someone of his calibre.*'

Left-sided Billy Askew, who had joined the club on trial, earned himself a permanent deal and Billy Woof, a former team-mate of Askew's at Middlesbrough, also signed for the Tigers whilst defender Bobby McNeil was another to join the club.

THE ROBINSON RENAISSANCE

The season did not start as planned with only one win from the first five games and, with an untried manager, certainly at league level, there was some disquiet amongst supporters. However, Appleton's philosophy was to build from the back and a strong defence letting in few goals was at the cornerstone of City's success under Appleton over the next couple of years.

Garreth Roberts remains a fan of Appleton's qualities as a manager, whatever his idiosyncrasies: *'Colin Appleton was brilliant with the younger players though he probably got on the nerves of the older lads. He was one for hundreds of meetings and because I was captain I was a sort of mediator between the manager and the players. So at the end of training he would come over to me and say that there was a meeting and I would get all the lads together as the bearer of bad news! So everyone got changed and we'd all be sat there in the home dressing room and Colin walks in, then you'd listen for maybe an hour. It was probably about 20 minutes but it felt like hours! You maybe wouldn't understand what the hell he was on about but then when you got home or started to think about it, maybe it seeped through.*

'He had meetings about everything you can think of and, lads being lads, we got out into the car park and used to ask each other if anyone understood a word of it! The attention span of a footballer is something like 10 minutes or something like that, you just want to go out and play, but something worked as we went from strength to strength, really.'

Jeff Radcliffe also had a lot of time for Appleton: *I respected Colin Appleton greatly for his knowledge of football. He used to have long team meetings that went on for an hour and he used to go off on all sorts of tangents. You looked at the faces of some of the players and it was priceless. Like Billy Askew, you knew that after about 30 seconds he was totally lost, hadn't a clue what he was on about! He did get the message across eventually but he went all around the houses to get there.*

'Colin could turn his hand to anything. I remember one year when he was at the club during the pre-season he re-panelled the dressing room. He was very knowledgeable and enthusiastic and

we used to joke that he carried his office in his jacket pocket because it was always bulging with things.'

Peter Skipper's return in time for the 1982-83 season was, in retrospect, crucial. Though he usually played left-back in his first spell at Boothferry Park, under Appleton he played as a centre-half and was a magnificent defensive rock. City's spine, with Norman in goal, Skipper in the centre of defence, Garreth Roberts in centre midfield and big Billy up front, was a formidable one and other positions were becoming settled too. Brian Marwood was developing into a quality right-sided forward and Steve McClaren was a skilful presence to have alongside Roberts in midfield. Also, his capture of Askew was looking inspired and the left midfielder was becoming one of the most skilful players to put on a black and amber shirt.

With a largely settled side, City soon put their indifferent early season form behind them and, after losing on the opening day of the season away at Bristol City, did not lose again until the end of October. City then went on a run of eight wins in eleven games to leave them firmly in the promotion places in time for the Christmas fixtures. Wimbledon were among City's main promotion challengers but a 2-1 win for the Tigers at Plough Lane put the Tigers on top of the table and looking set for their first promotion since 1965-66.

City stayed at the top for the rest of January but one or two defeats knocked the Tigers off the top of the table, notably a 1-0 loss at home to Tranmere, but that was to turn out to be the team's only home defeat of the season and by the end of March, a 1-0 victory over promotion rivals Port Vale, in front of 14,000, had City looking well set for promotion. There was time to introduce one or two notable loanees. John Hawley, who had left City in 1978 rejoined us on loan from Arsenal, playing three games and scoring one goal whilst Liverpool legend Emlyn Hughes, after his spell as Rotherham player-manager, ended his illustrious career at Boothferry Park.

It had been an eventful time for both City and Hawley since he last played in the black and amber and he remembered: *'I was at Arsenal and wasn't getting into the team and I think I went to Orient on loan, prior to coming back to City as Ken Knighton was manager. Terry Neill was the Arsenal manager and it was obviously the Hull City connection which would be why it came about.*

'I came back to what was one of the most bizarre set-ups I'd ever seen. Don Robinson wanted me to run out onto the pitch waving my arms about, which just wasn't me, and Colin Appleton was the weirdest man I've ever known! He'd call a meeting and we'd all sit there and he'd start talking about tactics and then go off on a tangent. He'd start talking to the apprentices who would be in the same room and he'd talk to them for about three-quarters of an hour while we'd all be just sitting there. It was bizarre, Robinson was a showman. Appleton, I wasn't there long enough to get to know him, but I'm not sure anyone got to know him.

'I came back to Boothferry Park on the first morning and I'd never been to a club where you didn't have your kit laid out. There was a big pile of kit on the table and you'd just help yourself. Everything had gone by this time because all the players had been in and got their kit so there was hardly anything left. So I looked through and found this real good shirt, because I was a big lad and not much fitted me, and a pair of shorts. I was fully kitted out and there were only about three kits left. I went back to the bench and someone says, "They're Billy's." So I put them back!'

The signing of Hughes, in time for the Port Vale home game, proved another wise move as his experience at the run-in stage ensured there were no jitters to affect the young side.

Don Robinson explained: *'Emlyn Hughes came in for half a season and he helped as he was that type of character who came in and helped the others along. He was the first big name player we'd had at the club for some time and he helped to regenerate the enthusiasm, it helped show that big things were happening.'*

At the rather less than salubrious Sealand Road, home of Chester, in front of just 2,500 - though there were about a thousand City fans in attendance - the Tigers secured promotion with a goalless draw, the first promotion since 1966. The revival had begun and Robinson's gamble with Appleton as manager seemed a masterstroke.

A settled squad - only 20 players were used throughout the campaign - was the key to the success. It was also a settled first eleven as six players - Skipper, Marwood, Mutrie, Garreth Roberts, Dale Roberts and McClaren - played 40 league games or more. With the side being so youthful, there was also the hope that the best was still to come from this team.

Garreth Roberts, a key member of the side, remembers the time with great affection: '*It was a young team growing up together and we were all pretty hungry as well. We all wanted to do well and for some others who had played league football before, like Tony Norman, it was their first chance to establish themselves as a first-teamer, so I think that along with Colin and Don, it all came together. It was just a quirk of fate that it all came together at one place at one time.*

'*The players were the main ones but we still needed Don Robinson taking us to Scarborough for a piss-up every now and then and it needed Colin Appleton doing his motivational chat and all this type of stuff. It doesn't come around very often but you only realise how good it was at that time years later when you are looking back.*'

Jeff Radcliffe also remembers it as a good time with both Don and Colin Appleton adding to the fun: '*It was an enjoyable time to be at the club. Both of them were great characters and there were some wonderful moments. The funniest thing I saw Colin Appleton do was in a nightclub in Gibraltar. Colin isn't a drinker but he had one or two that night and he was on this little dance floor with a glass of lager on his head dancing away. And of course he slipped and the lager went everywhere!*

'*Also in Gibraltar, he got everyone together and said we had a game in a couple of days, I don't mind you getting a bit of sun, but be careful not to burn your feet because if you do you won't get your boots on, so keep your feet covered. We went down to breakfast the following morning and Colin limps in, Dennis asked him what's up and he said he'd burnt his feet! Boothy said, "What a manager, not only does he tell you, he actually shows you what happens if you do it!"*'

Don Robinson himself enjoyed the experience and recognised the effect it was having in forging the team spirit which was to serve the club so well: '*Having been involved in sport in the past a lot of what we did was based on getting the team spirit right. We went on these foreign trips and if we went down to London we stayed in a good hotel. We didn't want to waste money but we were able to do deals. The team came over to Scarborough for two or three days and we put them up in the Royal Hotel and had dinner down there and a few speeches afterwards. These were young men bonding and they thought it was marvellous.'*

Season 1983-84

City got the new season off to a terrific start with a 4-1 win at home to Burnley, with a brace of goals each from Billy Whitehurst and new signing Steve Massey, and followed this up with an away win at Gillingham. The side was in great form and were not beaten until the twelfth game of the season, by which time Millwall 5-0 and Sheffield United 4-1 had also been mauled by the Tigers.

By the turn of the year, City had overcome a sticky October and were riding high, helped by an excellent Christmas period which saw them record four wins in a row, beating Bristol Rovers, Scunthorpe, Rotherham and Port Vale.

Early in the New Year fans were expected to turn out en masse to follow City to Burnley but despite many of the fans reaching their destination, the team failed to arrive.

The weather on the M62, a combination of snow, wind and ice, saw the coach swerve from side to side more than once on the hazardous journey. As the coach somehow arrived in West Yorkshire, the weather was still atrocious and Colin Appleton made a phone call to his Burnley counterpart, John Bond, from Hartshead Moor services. They were told that the Turf Moor pitch was playable and the weather in East Lancashire not as bad, but the City management had already decided that it was too dangerous to carry on with the journey and they informed Burnley of their decision, promptly turned round and set off back for Hull.

Garreth Roberts said: '*As the journey went on we didn't fancy it and we were having a go at the bus driver. As we were going the bus was swerving all over the road and we nearly went into a ditch a couple of times. So in the end we just accepted that we couldn't make it and turned round just before we got over the Pennines. Of course, we found out that a lot of our fans had managed to get there.'*

This unanimous decision did not go down well with the Football League who instigated an inquiry into the matter, with the club fretting over any resultant punishment, most notably the possible docking of points which would have affected the team's promotion push. Therefore, the club were grateful only to be fined and warned over their future conduct, and when they finally did get to Burnley the following May for the last game of the season, there was punishment of a different kind waiting for them.

As the season drew to a close, every game took on greater importance and City could have made virtually certain of Division Two football at Port Vale on a May Bank Holiday Monday evening following Sheffield United's 3-1 defeat at Bolton in the afternoon. City had no injury problems and Vale were missing a couple of key players but some bad decisions went against the Tigers in that game and there was also, in the words of Simon Redfern of the *Hull Daily Mail*, 'some inexplicable team selection' by Colin Appleton and City crucially went down to a 1-0 defeat. Redfern said in the *Mail*: *A draw seemed to be all that Appleton wanted from the match judging by the formation with which he began it. Whitehurst was at centre half and two defensive players, McEwan and Garry Swann, were battling in midfield. Also the City boss chose Marwood and Steve Massey up front to battle against a tall Port Vale defence.*

In addition, Billy Askew was not even given a place on the bench and City fans flooded the *Mail* offices with letters after the game, criticising Appleton's team selection and tactics.

The penultimate game of the season, at home to Bristol Rovers, gave the Tigers another opportunity to all but clinch promotion but the team were held to a frustrating 0-0 draw despite dominating practically the whole game. With Sheffield United winning their last game, it meant that City needed to win their last game, the rearranged trip to Burnley, by three clear goals to overtake Sheffield United and take the third promotion place.

THE ROBINSON RENAISSANCE

Garreth Roberts added: '*In the final game we knew exactly what we had to do. A couple of my mates who were Sheffield United players were in the crowd as well, obviously they all came over to see who was going to be promoted. We scored two goals fairly early on; Brian (Marwood) scored a couple. I remember I had a shot, beat the goalkeeper from about 15 or 16 yards out, but then their centre-half got in the way of it, it struck his knee and went over the bar. We thought that wouldn't matter but as the second half wore on we just couldn't get anywhere.*'

City won the game 2-0 and the lack of a third goal meant that Sheffield United hung on to third place by virtue of scoring more goals, 86 compared to City's 71, a heartbreaking way to end the season and many of the City players were in tears when they left the field. Somehow they managed to emerge from the dressing room to come out onto the pitch, to applaud the supporters who had made the trip and who had continued chanting after the final whistle.

Don Robinson was absent from the game. He explained: '*I was in London when the Burnley game was taking place. I had to look after my businesses and I was in the Climond Club which we owned in those days, one of London's most upmarket casinos, where the Kerry Packers of the world used to go. I said to the waiter, "Will you find the scores out for me?" I found out it was 2-0 and I got a bottle of champagne out. I couldn't believe it when I found out the final score, I was sure we'd go on to get four or five. It took me a week to get over it I was shattered.*'

However, the terrible night for a young team was to get even worse when their manager, who had nursed them through the last two seasons, told them he was quitting the club within minutes of them leaving the field.

Colin Appleton almost joined Swansea the previous December following John Toshack's resignation as their manager. However, he rejected their lucrative contract offer at that stage as he felt he still had a job to do at Boothferry Park. The Welsh club had not forgotten about him and were still keen to get him to go to South Wales. This time they succeeded, reportedly offering him double the salary he was getting at City.

LOOK BACK IN AMBER

Garreth Roberts adds: '*After the game we went back into the changing rooms and that's when Colin told us that he was resigning. We were all absolutely gutted but people went off in their own little areas of the changing room and just tried to take it in. It was a kick in the balls followed by a kick in the teeth.*'

Appleton himself said at the time: '*I couldn't do it before tonight because of the importance of the game but if we had gone up it wouldn't have made any difference. I had definitely made my mind up that it was time for a change. I won't be manager of Hull next season.*'

Don Robinson, shattered by the result, was still unaware of the further drama of the night. He explained: '*I only realised that Colin Appleton had resigned when I got back to my hotel and my son rang me at about eleven o'clock to tell me he'd gone. I couldn't believe it, it was one of the worst nights I had at Hull City because I thought he'd be so loyal to the club. I thought he was ill-advised or misled because he didn't make a success of the job at Swansea. I think Colin needed Chilton by his side with the two of them working as a team.*'

It was speculated that Appleton may have timed the announcement so that he did not have to face Don Robinson with the news but, whatever his reasons, the manner of his departure infuriated those connected with City. Simon Redfern of the *Daily Mail* wrote: *He could not have picked a worse moment apart from before the match and his timing showed a complete disregard for the depression from which the players and his assistant Chris Chilton were suffering. Surely Appleton could have waited until the dust had settled from Tuesday's setback or until the season was completely over before dropping the bombshell.*

With or without the manager, there were still the recriminations over the season which had just ended. To many the Burnley game was typical of a season in which the Tigers had suffered from a good deal of bad luck, having hit the woodwork many times and been the victims of some controversial refereeing decisions. However, City in some ways had themselves to blame as they had plenty of chances to score important goals throughout the season and too often they went begging. They failed to score in eleven league games, quite a high number for a team hoping to get promotion. As in the previous campaign it was the defence which was responsible for the team's success and City had the best defensive record in the division with 19 clean sheets.

The players had little time to ponder on the events at Burnley before they were due to fly to America for a post-season tour organised by Don Robinson. The chairman put Dennis Booth in charge of the team for the trip where they were due to face the Tampa Bay Rowdies.

Though few players probably felt like it after such a traumatic end to a season, the City squad duly flew out to the United States.

Garreth Roberts said: '*With hindsight it was a great move by Don Robinson to take us to the States at the end of that season. We were all fed up, it was quite a long tour and because of the way the season finished we weren't really looking forward to it but when we got there with the sun on our backs, playing in some brilliant stadiums over there, we all got back together again and regrouped.*

'*We had a good time over there. I remember us playing golf and we went out in about seven or eight of these golfing buggy things. I think only two came back because we got so bored with the golf we didn't bother getting out of the buggy to hit the shots. We were swinging the club with one hand and driving the buggy with the other! There were quite a few hills and streams along the course and we flew at it in these buggies racing each other!*'

One player who didn't go on the trip was Brian Marwood. City fans knew that if the club failed to win promotion at Burnley, then Marwood would not be staying, he was too much of a talent to be playing Third Division football and supporters knew he was destined for great things. A few days after the Burnley game he was placed on the transfer list at his own request, stating that he had a verbal agreement with the chairman which stated that if City failed to get promotion, he would be allowed to leave the club.

Robinson explained: '*Brian Marwood came to see me at the end of the season that we got promoted to the Third Division and said that he would play for us for another season. He said he wanted to play in the First Division but that he wanted that to be with Hull City, so he would play on for us. It showed the team spirit we had at City because he could have gone then and nobody would have thought any less of him. When we failed to go up it was obvious that Brian would go and it was only fair to him. He went on to have a successful career and I was very pleased for him.'*

Inevitably he was sold, to Sheffield Wednesday for £115,000 in the summer, a complete steal, though it could have been worse as there were strong rumours that Sheffield United were interested. For Marwood to have headed to Bramall Lane after they beat City to promotion would have been the ultimate kick in the teeth and would also have affected the goodwill that Marwood had built up with City fans. As it was, Wednesday won the bidding, albeit at a ridiculous price.

Marwood was, not surprisingly, a huge success at Wednesday and was sold to Arsenal, even making a brief substitute appearance for England. He donated his shirt from that game to Dennis Booth, his great friend and mentor at City who had done so much to help him in his professional career.

So, with Marwood gone, Robinson had another problem as he searched for a new manager. Early favourites for the manager's job in the days after Appleton's departure were Chris Chilton, Jack Charlton and Colin Murphy, boss at Lincoln City. However, Robinson eventually settled on Brian Horton as player-manager, City's first since Terry Neill.

Don Robinson explains: '*Jack Charlton was a very good friend of mine, a great character as well as a World Cup winner. So I rang him and offered him the job. He asked for a couple of days to think about it and he rang back saying he didn't want to get back into management and suggested Brian Horton. So I arranged to meet Brian in York and, from what Jack had said about him, the job was his if he wanted it. As it turned out it was the right thing at the right time for the club. He was strict on discipline and a good coach and we won promotion. Again, all of Brian, Chillo and Dennis Booth who had come in on the coaching side, all got on to form a good team.'*

Horton joined the Tigers following a successful playing career with Port Vale, Brighton and Luton Town and he came with an excellent reputation as a leader on the pitch. Ironically, Colin Appleton had wanted to sign Horton as a player the previous season and with such a young and upcoming squad, a signing of that type may well have made a big impact as, talented though the team was, an older head in the middle of the park was perhaps required when things did not always go to plan.

The new manager faced a difficult job trying to ensure that the team approached the new season in the right manner. Most supporters felt a 'hangover' from the night at Turf Moor and it would have been surprising if the players didn't also. However, it was a help to have a new face in the dug out and Horton took to his first managerial job well.

Garreth Roberts said: '*When a new manager comes in that gets you motivated also. You have to pull your socks up. Even though I was a regular and captain you're looking to prove yourself all over again. I respected him as well because he was a midfield player, similar sort of style to myself. He was good for us and didn't change the team very much when he first came in.*'

Season 1984-85

Alan Taylor had left the club along with Brian Marwood but the majority of the squad was unchanged. Dennis Booth was not retained as a player but had his job on the coaching staff at the club whilst Billy Whitehurst, Garreth Roberts, Bobby McNeil, Gary Swann, Ian Davis and Paul Ollson were all offered new terms.

Three new signings were brought in by Horton in preparation for the new season. Lawrie Pearson came from Gateshead, Mike Ring from Ballymena and Neil Williams from Watford as the new boss looked to erase the Burnley game from the players' memory.

City got off to a solid, unspectacular start to the new season and the team were settled in mid-table throughout August and September. City were still 'feeling their way' into the new season but as late as November, the team were still frustratingly inconsistent, lying in twelfth place.

A promotion challenge was not yet apparent but the team got into their stride between late October and the beginning of January when they went 12 games without defeat, including eight wins, to propel them towards the top of the table.

The season contained two remarkable comeback games showing the spirit within the side, most notably at Orient. Orient went three-up inside the first half an hour and most thought that was game over, with the four hundred City fans wondering whether to leave the ground early. Billy Askew got the Tigers back into the game direct from a corner at the end of the first half but Barry Silkman scored from 25 yards to make it 4-1.

With only 25 minutes left the best City could hope for was another consolation goal to make the score look respectable. However, goals from Steve Massey and Andy Flounders brought it back to 3-4 and Orient were looking worried. With thirteen minutes left City got a penalty which Stan McEwan scored to put City on level terms. That would have been quite an achievement but Andy Flounders scored in the 88th minute to seal an incredible victory amid wild celebrations from the City fans who were lucky enough to be at Brisbane Road.

Another only slightly less remarkable comeback was witnessed by more City fans, at home to Derby County. City were two goals down with 20 minutes left but they still had time to have a man sent off and score the three goals needed for another incredible victory. Whitehurst, with two, and Flounders got the goals.

The team was a settled one, as virtually all successful ones are and, equally importantly, had a great spine. Tony Norman was in goal, Skipper and McEwan at the centre of defence, Garreth Roberts anchored the midfield with Billy Askew supplying the creativity and Big Billy was up front, assisted by Andy Flounders who had probably his best season at City. Brian Horton himself played in about half the league games that season.

It was the transformation of Whitehurst that was the most remarkable. His first games in a black and amber shirt were not too far short of embarrassing. He had the work-rate but patently lacked skill and a return to non-league appeared likely. However, slowly and surely, during his time at Boothferry Park, Whitehurst improved to such an extent that it was no surprise that scouts began to appear in the Best Stand on a regular basis with the intent of running the rule over City's number nine.

THE ROBINSON RENAISSANCE

Garreth Roberts said: *'Billy was a raw talent when he came to City, he couldn't trap a bag of cement as they say, but he probably thought that he had to make it as a footballer. He didn't want to go back down the pit or back in the builder's yard, wherever he'd come from. So when he started here his first touch was poor and his positional play wasn't good but he listened to Chillo. Chillo used to get him coming in at the far post and using his bulk and he made a great career in the end.'*

Whitehurst was a central figure in one of the other key games of that season. Bradford and City were both competing for promotion, with both eventually achieving it, though Bradford's triumph was tragically cut short by the fire which killed so many supporters on the last day of the season. In the February, nearly 15,000 came to Boothferry for a game between the two teams and the eventual champions won by two goals to nil, quite an achievement considering that they played for most of the game with a stand-in goalkeeper, Eric McManus being carried off after being splattered around the goalpost by Whitehurst!

Defender Richard Jobson was signed by Horton in February 1985, along with Mick Hollifield, in a bid to strengthen the defence in time for the vital run-in, but the 21-year-old Hull-born player who was signed from Watford, gained an unwanted habit of going AWOL.

He failed to turn up for the match against Bristol Rovers because he was homesick, quite ironic as he was born in Hull, and then compounded the problem by failing to turn up a second time, this for a reserve match. He was fined two weeks' wages and Brian Horton was losing patience with a player who was running out of chances at Boothferry Park. Horton said: *'I understand his problems which are concerned with moving house, and other personal details. I accepted it the first time, but I can't accept it anymore - the club is bigger than any one individual.'*

Jobson played in relatively few games that season, his best for City was still to come, but the team were progressing well without him. City lost away at Gillingham at the end of February but then went on a fantastic run of 12 wins in 15 games, the final victory securing promotion with a 1-0 win away at Walsall with a goal scored by Pete Skipper. It was a wonderful run of form and promotion was a great achievement after the way in which it was denied to City the season before.

Horton also received praise from his predecessor as City manager. Colin Appleton returned to Boothferry Park to watch City lose to York City once promotion had been confirmed and backed Horton to take the club further. He said: *'He's done tremendous work. You don't get the results if you don't make a majority of good decisions. The season had been all about keeping the club on the right lines.'*

Season 1985-86

A look at the fixture list for the following season showed what we had been missing during our extended stay in the wilderness,. Portsmouth at home closely followed by a trip to Elland Road. Bradford City moved up with us to make seven Yorkshire teams in the Second Division that season if Middlesbrough were to be included and Don Robinson left no one in any doubt as to his intentions for City. He said at the time, 'We want to go straight through the Second Division and on to aim towards Europe.'

Despite the hyperbole, Robinson was enjoying his role as chairman and, as with so many, saw his weekend mood dictated by how City did on Saturday afternoon.

'If we lost and I was driving home from City on a Saturday night, I didn't want to go out. I took it personally and got emotionally involved which is how it should be, that's how you get enjoyment out of it. A lot of people today are involved in football purely for the financial aspect but I wasn't although I still wanted to make City profitable as a matter of pride.'

Brian Horton had lost Steve McClaren who, despite wanting to move to a First Division club, moved backwards, if only for a season, by joining Third Division Derby County. Added to the squad were Frankie Bunn, Bobby Doyle, Garry Parker and Pat Heard but despite these acquisitions, the team took some time to settle into life back in the Second Division. The first six league games saw four draws and two losses and City were struggling near the bottom of the table but worries were eased as City won the next two matches, both at home, seeing off Millwall 3-0 and Carlisle 4-0.

City's best spell came over the Christmas period when City had a run of six wins from nine games, losing just once which included a perfect January winning all three league games against Barnsley, Bradford and Oldham. However, apart from that run, City failed to string a number of wins together in a bid to put pressure on the teams above them and hovered near to the promotion places without ever looking likely to get into the top three.

The season ended well with victories over Norwich and Brighton to ensure that City finished in sixth position. Only twice had the club finished higher than sixth spot in the Second Division and only a few too many home draws had cost City a higher position. Still, the Tigers finished the season as the top club in Yorkshire, ahead of Leeds and Sheffield United.

City managed this with a squad of just 19 players and six of the first team regulars had been playing with the club in the Fourth Division just three seasons before. Horton had paid just £145,000 for Bunn, Doyle, Parker and Heard but City recouped the money, receiving £230,000 from Newcastle United for Billy Whitehurst halfway through the season.

The season was also notable for the Tigers scoring 65 goals, though many of those came before the sale of Whitehurst and City struggled to make the same impact up front when the big target man left. Frankie Bunn was City's top scorer with 20 whilst Andy Flounders got 13. Meanwhile, Bunn, Stan McEwan and Tony Norman were all ever-presents in the league campaign.

The club had travelled a long way in a short time and Garreth Roberts believes that Horton himself deserves much credit. He recalls: '*Brian was a good manager and his motivation was unbelievable, which had an effect on the players. I remember him pinning me against a wall once! One of the things we used to do was watch our weekend matches again on the following Monday afternoon on video. It was boring as hell watching 90 minutes of football but it was there to highlight the things that went wrong. I remember we drew with Leicester 2-2 and I scored and so I thought I'd be okay for the Monday afternoon video. They scored and so he said, "Whose fault was that?" and stopped the video. It looked like a good goal to me but he went round the room asking everybody. And someone on the other side said out of the blue, "It was your fault Garreth," and Brian agreed, saying that I should have been covering.*

'I think I said something to Brian like "Oh you get so fucking intense you do," and his eyes popped out of his head and he pinned me up against the wall, giving me the old finger in the chest, saying "I'll show you what intense is!" Some of the lads were looking at me as if to ask, what does intense mean?!'

Jeff Radcliffe remembers the intensity, but adds that the right chemistry in the management team meant it was a good time for the club: '*It was a good era because Brian could be tough, one of the old style, chucking teacups and the like but he had Boothy who was a great foil for him, a born comedian. So Brian would slag them off and then Boothy would put an arm round them and get them geed up for the next game. Brian was a good manager which he's proving again at Macclesfield.*'

City went off for a week in Marbella in good heart, having had one of the most successful seasons in the club's history and hoping that perhaps the club could go one better the season after.

Season 1986-87

The new campaign got off to a terrible start with Bobby Doyle, who had been so influential in midfield for City, breaking his leg in a pre-season 'friendly' with Doncaster. His presence was badly missed as the season began and after victories over West Brom and Millwall, City lost three of the next four matches and a winless December and January saw City battling against relegation.

After Christmas, City spent the whole time in the bottom six and by February the team was desperately in need of new blood to stave off the threat of the drop. It came when Horton signed two players, forward Alex Dyer from Blackpool and defender Charlie Palmer, who had been languishing in Derby reserves.

Palmer's impact was immediate. His arrival meant that Horton could reshuffle the defence with Palmer slotting in at right-back, enabling Richard Jobson to move into his best position in the centre of defence. 1986-87 saw the emergence of Richard Jobson as a centre-half of real quality. After having spent a couple of years at City as a utility defender who had also played in midfield on occasions, he found his place alongside Pete Skipper and when he did, in 18 matches, City conceded just 12 goals. He also made a valuable contribution at the other end of the field, scoring six goals from set-pieces.

In the end, with a strong finishing burst, City were safe from any lingering relegation worries, finishing in 14th place. They also finished the season as the Second Division's side in form with just two defeats in their last 16 league games and but for a few more goals to turn draws into victories, could have even been challenging for a play-off spot in the first year of their introduction. The big problem, in contrast to the previous season, had been a shortage of goals with just 41 scored and Andy Saville was the leading scorer with just nine in the league.

City had a little success in the FA Cup, beating Shrewsbury and Swansea to face Wigan at Springfield Park in the fifth round. It was an excellent chance to make the quarter-finals for the first time since 1970-71 as Wigan were lower league opposition, but City's league form going into the match was poor and the Tigers performed badly on the day, losing the tie 3-0. Brian Horton had been largely immune from criticism as City manager, but his substitution in this game was booed loudly as Billy Askew, one of the few City players to emerge from the game with any credit, was replaced by Andy Flounders. The City side that day was Norman, Palmer, Pearson, Jobson, Skipper, Parker, Williams, Dyer, Saville, Askew and Roberts.

Horton's priority for the following season was a proven goalscorer and a replacement for Bobby Doyle as a defensive midfield player. Horton gave free transfers to John Davies, Lawrie

LOOK BACK IN AMBER

Pearson, Steve Brentano and Paul Ollson but both Stan McEwan and Garry Parker were on the transfer list after asking for a move.

Horton also looked to freshen up the coaching side and, after letting Chris Chilton leave the club, brought in Tom Wilson, who had been a distinguished centre-half for the club between 1967 and 1971. Wilson remembers: *'I had been doing the football academy, school of excellence part-time in the gym on a Tuesday and Thursday night with Dave King, coaching the lads in preparation for them becoming juniors and Dave recommended me to Brian Horton when he was looking for someone to take over the reserve team. At that time I think there was a parting of the ways between Chris Chilton and the club over some matter so I slotted into that position. Thankfully there was no animosity between me and Chris and he wished me all the best. So I was back at the club permanently as reserve team manager and youth team coach.*

'The players in the juniors at the time included Andy Payton, Neil Buckley, Gavin Kelly, Leigh Jenkinson, Dean Windass and Mike Smith so it was a very good side. In fact that very first year we also had players like Andy Saville, Nicky Brown and Paul Olsson. We were in the Hull and District Premier League, which is a hell of a league, and won it with lads who were under 18. The next year the juniors went into the league containing sides like Middlesbrough and Newcastle.'

Tom felt that the club was in safe hands under Brian Horton, adding: *'Brian was absolutely terrific to work with, an honest, straightforward, face-to-face guy who, if he had anything to say to you, would say it to your face, whether it was good, bad or indifferent. He ran the club from top to bottom, knowing everybody from the tea lady right up to the chairman. He spoke to almost everyone at the club every day and always had time for people.*

'The club at the time was on a very sound footing right through from the coaching side onwards and the scouting system he had introduced was incredible. At that time Dave King was head teacher in one of the schools in Hull and through his contacts he had almost every schoolboy game covered weekly, so we knew all the top lads in the Hull area who were coming through virtually before anybody else had recognised them and through that we were

able to sign them up for the School of Excellence or the academy. We got a lot of decent lads for virtually nothing, who played for the club and left to make the club some money.'

Tom joined a coaching team still including Dennis Booth whose impact on the club went beyond his coaching ability. John Cooper remembers him fondly: *'Dennis is still missed and personalities like Dennis bring it all together. I can understand why he got on very well with Brian Horton because Brian was the manager and Dennis would lighten it up a little bit. My lasting memory of him, apart from always nicking Freddie Cowell's cap and throwing it all over the place, was my birthday, my first year working with him.*

'I was on the pitch and Dennis came up to me and said, "John, chairman, telephone." I'd been briefed about Dennis's antics so I said, "No, I'm not coming." "Seriously, he wants you, it's about the fertiliser you ordered," and it was ironic because I had literally done a deal for some fertiliser, so I thought I had to go and see if the chairman really did want to speak to me.

'I went and as soon as I got into the tunnel I was ambushed by all the kids and the old bath in the dressing room was full to the brim of ice cold water. This was in January so it was a freezing day as well. They carried me head high down the tunnel and Dennis said to the lads in a mock stern way, "Now lads, don't you throw Mr Cooper into that bath!" I said, "Please let me take my watch and my shoes off." That's part of the club that I miss. It's distanced itself now since those days but it's moved on.'

Martin Fish was invited onto the board by Don Robinson after working for the club when it went into receivership and then producing a share register which prompted Robinson to ask him to become a director. Fish saw that, despite the board including Christopher Needler, Richard Chetham, Mick Thorpe, Clifford Waite and Martin St Quinton, in reality the 'board' started and ended with one man, Don himself, with the others not heavily involved in the running of the club: *'Don was a bit of an eccentric, I like the guy, I think a lot of him and he fitted in with football in a certain way and the fans loved him but inevitably with an eccentric you are going to get these certain things, so he found board meetings very uninteresting. He wanted to see the financial information, wanted to know what was going on generally, but that was it and after an hour or so he had had enough. He wasn't a man with paper, he just said what he thought and that was it. So he ran the club himself because that was what he wanted to do.*

'He had bought the situation from Christopher Needler and thought he would run it his way. He wanted board members there to do other things for him because I remember I brought management accounts in. The board had never seen monthly management accounts before and I was amazed.'

The other directors also saw relatively little of the manager of the day with Robinson having most contact with Brian Horton. Fish adds: '*I didn't have much contact with Brian Horton because Don was very much his own man and he tended to look after the manager, but I always got on with Brian fine when I came into contact with him. He came to the board meeting or the part of the board meeting to do with the playing side but he wasn't a man to ask for a lot of money, maybe because if you asked Don Robinson for a lot of money you wouldn't get it. Don was very careful in his dealings.*'

Don Robinson himself admits that the idea of a true board was not something which appealed to him. He was the chairman and the buck stopped with him. He said: '*We had a board but only held board meetings every couple of months. We were winning on the field, we were financially sound and everyone was happy and that was how it should be. In terms of hiring managers, that was my job. Someone had to be in overall control or else nothing would get done. I think that's how Adam Pearson does the job at the club now and he's doing a very good job.*

'*However, I did have a good board at the time. Martin was there and Mick Thorpe and Clifford Waite came on the board. Clifford was a City fanatic and I made him vice-chairman and he had his finger on the pulse of what the fans were feeling.*'

PART FOUR

New era, same old problems

Season 1987-88

The 1987-88 season began frustratingly with City letting slip a 2-0 lead at Boothferry Park to draw 2-2 with Blackburn. Two decent away draws followed at Stoke and Crystal Palace before City got their first win, beating Aston Villa 2-1 at home. Villa got their goal aided by the referee for what was probably the most ridiculous penalty I have ever seen, but though angered by conceding a goal under such circumstances, the players didn't lose their rag, but began to control the game and goals by Pat Heard and a superb individual effort by Alex Dyer saw the Tigers home.

A draw at Swindon followed by a home win over Bournemouth left City unbeaten as we travelled to Elland Road to take on Leeds. We had made a great start to the new season and Leeds were struggling but it was still a tall order to take on Leeds in front of their own fans.

Unlike the two previous years when we had been at the bottom of the Lowfields Stand, where the atmosphere had been affected, for this game we were given the whole of the South Stand which was far better for making some noise.

It soon became apparent that the team were just as fired up as the City fans. City held Leeds at bay until half-time and then our superiority showed with two sublime goals in front of the City fans. The goals, from Parker and Dyer, who was on his way to becoming a City legend, saw us win the game 2-0 in front of a surprisingly small Leeds crowd of just 18,000 and City were in the top three in the Second Division. Further victories over Oldham, Manchester City, Ipswich, Barnsley and Huddersfield cemented our place towards the top of the division and the scene was set for the Tigers to battle for the top spot in the division, against Terry Dolan's Bradford City.

A big Boothferry Park crowd of over 15,000 saw the top two in the division battle out a scoreless draw in a game of relatively few chances. City's form just about held up over the Christmas period and by the time we completed the double over Leeds, beating them 3-1 at Boothferry Park, we were into January and hoping that a successful start to 1988 would give us a real chance of First Division football.

However, the win over Leeds merely signalled the start of an alarming slump that eventually cost Brian Horton his job. From January 3 until the end of the season, City won just one more game, at home to Huddersfield, a wretched 17-game run which would have led to the club being relegated had we not had the excellent start to the season.

Brian Horton tried to make changes in a bid to resurrect the season; Leigh Jenkinson and Andy Payton were drafted into the first team from the reserves and the manager made a handful of new signings around the time of the transfer deadline. Ken DeMange was signed from Liverpool reserves, Wayne Jacobs came from Sheffield Wednesday, former international winger Peter Barnes was signed on loan from Manchester City and Keith Edwards returned to the club after a seven-year absence, joining City from Aberdeen. However, the new signings didn't reinvigorate a season which, after such an outstanding start, was turning into a real disappointment.

Don Robinson decided he had seen enough and, after an especially poor 4-2 home defeat to Swindon Town, he decided to sack Brian Horton.

Martin Fish remembers the sacking of Horton, saying: '*It was Don's decision alone to get rid of Brian Horton. The board meeting was literally in the directors' box while the game was going on. He whispered over to Chris Needler and said, "I think I've had enough, I think I'm going to get rid of Horton." That passed to me in the next row down and Mick Thorpe, who went mad and said that we should have a board meeting at the end of the game. But at the final whistle Don had gone down to the tunnel, in the dressing room and that was it, he did it on impulse as he did a lot of things.*'

Tom Wilson also remembers that night well: '*We'd played at Bradford on the Saturday and on the Sunday evening we were all supposed to go down to London for the PFA awards, including Don. So Dennis, Brian, myself and Don were all due to go down either on the Saturday evening or the Sunday morning. Trevor Cherry was manager at Bradford at the time and we were having a drink with him after the game and Don came bursting in, again impulsive, saying he wanted us to cancel going down to London because we had lost. Brian said don't be silly, we had just lost a game which had been close.*

'Don said that he wanted all the players in for training on the Sunday morning but Brian said it wouldn't make any difference to the result and we were playing again on the Tuesday night so they would be back in for training on the Monday morning. So Don didn't come with us to London and that may have made things a bit worse for Brian on the Tuesday night.'

Tom continued: *Almost immediately after Don Robinson sacked Brian Horton he felt he had made a mistake. That night we played Swindon and lost 4-2 at home, Dave Bamber and big Jimmy Quinn scored the goals. From the game finishing, Dennis Booth used to go into the dressing room first and Brian would follow and I used to wait until all the players were in. As I was coming off from the pitch you would turn left to go into the home dressing room. Brian's office was just past on the right. As I was passing his office, Don came out in a bit of a scurry and went into the dressing room. Brian called me in and said, "Tom, can you go and get Denise (*Brian's wife*), he just sacked me."*

'I said, "You're joking," but he was serious and asked again, "Would you go and get Denise? Don't tell her, just bring her down please." So I went upstairs and at the time Don Robinson's boardrooms were big and full of guests, he was a great host. After all these people trying to stop me for a chat I found Denise and took her downstairs. When I got downstairs, just to go into Brian's office, Don was coming out again. So he had been into the dressing room and had been back into Brian's office in the time it took me to get Denise and bring her downstairs.

'When I went in with Denise, he said, "You'll never guess what, he's only offered me my job back." He said, "I've told him to stuff it, he's hurt my pride. I couldn't work for him now." What had happened is that Don had gone into the dressing room and told the players what he'd done. They couldn't believe it and said to him that it was themselves that he ought to be sacking and straight away he had realised that he had been too impulsive, so he went

back to Brian and offered him his job back. Of course by then it was too late and sadly that was the start of things starting to go wrong.'

Despite the poor form going into the Swindon game, most supporters were shocked by Horton's departure. He was the manager who had taken us up to the Second Division and had established the club in the league. For most of that season, at least up until the New Year, we were a real threat though the lack of a '20-goal a season man' undoubtedly hindered our progress.

Don Robinson gave his own account of that night: *'Brian was married and he and his wife had been trying for children. They had twins and had been awake every night through that, so he looked tired and that was one of the reasons that we parted.*

'There wasn't a fall-out when he left; he did a piece in a paper recently saying how well he'd been treated at City and said that I put a cheque in his pocket for the rest of his contract, whereas other clubs wouldn't have dealt with him as honourably. I saw him recently when Port Vale played at Scarborough and it was like seeing a long-lost brother, he came straight up and gave me a hug and a kiss on the cheek. He's rung me a few times to ask about players he thought I might have seen.'

Dennis Booth stayed to lead the club until the end of the season as caretaker-manager - he was assisted in that role by Tom Wilson - and most felt that Booth would be offered the manager's job on a permanent basis during the summer.

That feeling that Dennis would become permanent manager gained further ground when he was given permission to pay out £100,000 for Watford's central defender Steve Terry during the early part of the summer, but Don Robinson had another surprise up his sleeve when he announced, in June 1988, that Eddie Gray was to be City's new manager. Gray still had a good reputation in the game though his management spell in charge of Leeds ended in disappointment. On leaving Leeds, he took up the manager's job at Rochdale before joining the Tigers.

Don Robinson explains the appointment: *'Dennis Booth did a very good job for Hull City, but I think sometimes you can be too close to a situation that you don't see the whole picture. He was a great guy but I felt he was too close to the club and I needed someone from the outside coming in, which is why Eddie became manager.*

'Eddie Gray had been at Rochdale and to me was something of a hero. I had done no research on him really; it was just me with his name in my head. I rang him from Harrogate one day and offered him the job and he asked for a couple of days to think about it. Since then I've thought that if he couldn't make up his mind immediately then it obviously wasn't right for him or the club.

'Also, part of the deal was that he didn't want to live in Hull and again that should have alerted me at the time, because it's important that the manager should be a real part of the club by living in the area. He lived in Wetherby and it's too far away to do the job effectively. You have to be part of the community, a part of the fans, and you can't do that when you're living so far away.'

Season 1988-89

From the sometimes fierce Brian Horton, Eddie Gray was a different manager altogether, closer to the Ken Houghton style, according to Jeff Radcliffe: 'Eddie was a lovely man, one of the fittest guys at the club. In pre-season training they used to run around Beverley Westwood and he was always in the first three. Put him in the gym with a football, nobody could get the ball off him. Again, he was so nice, possibly too nice to be the best football manager.'

Apart from Terry, City had two other debutants, Lee Warren and John Moore, both bought in by Gray, when they took on Manchester City in the first game of the new season. In a one-sided game in which City were completely outplayed, Keith Edwards scored to give City a very lucky first-day win. However, the win was a flash in the pan and 1988-89 was destined to be a season of struggle. City only managed another three wins in the next two months with good away victories at Portsmouth and Shrewsbury, as well as a 3-0 home win over Chelsea.

NEW ERA, SAME OLD PROBLEMS

Terry had, by this time, cemented a place in the starting eleven and the player to lose out was Pete Skipper, who many thought was unfortunate to be frozen out of the first team picture. However, at 31, he couldn't wait around in the hope of a recall and Oldham were the lucky recipients, getting him for a bargain £40,000. The season saw more comings and goings with Alex Dyer, who had looked great the season before, going to Crystal Palace for £225,000.

City were lower mid-table going into December and, having the unusual position of no game from December 10 until Boxing Day, City used the opportunity to take a break. Don Robinson explained: '*We had a fortnight off in the league so I decided to take the team off to Bermuda! Of course, I'd opened my big mouth and told the players but Eddie said that it was his decision whether to go or not and he didn't want to go. I thought that with it being in December, it would do the players good but Eddie wasn't having it. So that put another doubt in my mind.*'

Both men stood their ground and eventually the team went off to Bermuda without the manager, winning two and drawing the other match on the short visit. Shortly after their return, it became clear that Eddie Gray had been busy in their absence as there was more transfer news to announce.

Tony Norman had been bought into the club by Mike Smith for what many at the time thought was an inflated price of £30,000. In hindsight it showed that whatever faults Mike Smith may have had, he could spot talent. Norman, 442 appearances for City later, had become, to many, City's best-ever keeper, staying throughout the receivership time and remaining to play a crucial part in the team's revival under Colin Appleton and then Brian Horton. News that he was to be sold was hard for many to take as he had become such a favourite with fans and it was hard to imagine anybody else being in goal for the Tigers. However, Sunderland came in with a bid of £400,000 and offered two players to City in part-exchange.

Ian Hesford came as replacement goalkeeper and Billy Whitehurst made a welcome return to Boothferry Park after an unhappy time at Newcastle and mixed fortunes at Oxford, Reading and Roker Park. The return of Whitehurst placated the fans who were undoubtedly upset at Norman's departure, especially as he admitted he didn't want to leave.

LOOK BACK IN AMBER

But Whitehurst was back and before he and Hesford played in the home draw with Ipswich (Whitehurst inevitably scored), graffiti on the top of the North Terrace hailed the return of the hero, reading 'Billy is back!' Hesford seemed an adequate replacement for Norman, at least initially, and the return of the Edwards/Whitehurst partnership saw a revival in the Tigers fortunes over the next few weeks. We beat Barnsley away, Bournemouth 4-0 at home - helped by an Edwards hat-trick - and also won away at Leicester.

As Whitehurst was back in black and amber, the supporters were ready to wave goodbye to John Moore who had become another of the 'Boothferry boo-boys' favourite targets. He had scored the winning goal in a 1-0 win over Swindon Town and most City fans would have hoped that would have kick-started his stalling career with the Tigers, but most knew in their hearts that it would never happen. He only played another four games for the club before being placed on the transfer-list.

As the New Year approached City were still in lower mid-table in Division Two but with all the transfer activity, at least Gray was moulding Horton's team into one more in his own name. It was also a good time to be at Boothferry Park according to those who worked with Eddie. Tom Wilson said: '*Eddie was so laid back; he was one of the breed of footballers who was so good as a player that they find it difficult to become a good manager. You think of Bobby Moore and Bobby Charlton as good players but not great managers and Eddie was kind of in that mould when he came to us. He was like a player when he came here, he took part in training and was up at the front leading with the running. He was certainly at the front leading with the talent in five-a-side matches in the gym or with stuff like that.*

'*I think Eddie's difficulty was accepting the players' ability on our books at the time. Even at the age he was when he came to Hull he was still a hell of a player, and he had been a great player, so he came to a Second Division club where the players were obviously a little inferior to what he had at Leeds in his prime. He told me that they haven't got the ability and no matter what we say in this game, it isn't going to make any difference.*'

NEW ERA, SAME OLD PROBLEMS

Garreth Roberts also enjoyed his brief time working under Eddie Gray: '*Eddie was a great bloke and the respect we had for him was unbelievable because he was a Scottish international and we'd seen all the clips on the TV about his dribbling with the ball, and you could only respect the guy. He was still as fit as anything, the main thing I remember about Eddie is that he used to come in before us for training and do a 12-minute run. He used to do all his training before ours started at 10 o'clock and when we did pre-season running he was always at the front. You used to have to work hard to beat the manager, he was that fit.*

'*Also, he was really thoughtful about your family. So he'd always ask me about the wife and children and knew them all by name. He led us at the time we played Liverpool so we had a good cup run that season, but after that we died a death for the rest of the season. He didn't really get the chance here but he was good with the older players and knew that the man-management side had to be spot-on with more experienced players.*'

Though the league form was disappointing, Gray's season in charge will be remembered mainly for the cup run that year. First we overcame Cardiff in a tricky away tie in the Third Round before facing Bradford City at Valley Parade in the Fourth. It was the time of the inflatables that never really caught on as it should at Boothferry Park and on the day that Grimsby took thousands of Harry Haddocks down to First Division Wimbledon, we had the odd tiger in with about 2,000 City fans on the away terrace at Valley Parade. For me, living in Bradford at the time and knowing so many Bradford fans, it was an unforgettable game. Billy Whitehurst scored in the first few minutes with a fantastic 25-yard shot and in the second half, Edwards finished it off with another wonderful finish in front of the City fans to give City a memorable win. Bradford also had future Tiger Leigh Palin sent off after an incident with Garreth Roberts.

The Monday lunchtime cup draw incredibly gave the Tigers the tie of the round as Liverpool came out of the hat with the tie to be played at Boothferry Park. The team of Dalglish, Lawrenson, Barnes, Hansen and Rush were champions and the best team in the country and Hull, for the first time in many years, truly did go cup crazy.

105

LOOK BACK IN AMBER

The week before the cup tie, Shrewsbury came to Hull and, with vouchers to get tickets for the following week's cup tie on offer, a crowd of over 11,000 turned up with queues forming down North Road to get in through the turnstiles, scenes which hadn't been witnessed at Boothferry Park since the late 1960s. City produced a good performance, beating Shrewsbury 3-0, but most of the crowd didn't see it as at least half the crowd had left the ground at half-time to queue outside the ticket office which opened after the final whistle.

I was lucky enough to have a membership card so easily got a ticket but standing with my dad, a season ticket holder at Blundell Park, and my brother, hardly a City die-hard, whilst it was exciting seeing City in a real glamour tie, it was hard to avoid the feeling that the game had been 'hijacked' by people who were more interested in seeing the great Liverpool side than City and the possibility of being witness to a 'giant-killing'.

Though City were leading 2-1 at half-time, my own memory has Liverpool as always being in control and they duly finished the tie off early in the second half.

Tom Wilson, reserve team manager at the time, remembers the dressing room at half-time in the game. '*Against Liverpool in the cup we were 2-1 up at half-time and Dennis and I were quite anxious to consolidate. It was Liverpool with Barnes and Rush all playing and Eddie wanted to go 3-1 up. His aim was to go out in the second half and attack them but I was brought up with a defensive mentality at Millwall where we defended and if you won 1-0 that was fine. Eddie still wanted to attack and of course we lost the game 3-2, as we all know.*'

Don Robinson remembers the game as much for financial reasons as others: '*We were the first club ever to do a beam-back facility with the Liverpool game when it was shown to Liverpool fans at Anfield for those who couldn't get in to Boothferry Park. As for the game itself, if I'm honest the Liverpool game was the only one that I wasn't that keen for us to win, I would rather have drawn, get the 43,000 in over at Anfield and the tills would have been ticking over.*'

The 'special day' and almost inevitable 'creditable defeat' came and went but rarely has a game apparently had such an effect on a season. At the time of the game we were in fourteenth place (of course) but in a good vein of form. There was the potential to get into the play-offs with eighteen games left, but instead the team slid rapidly down the league, winning just one more game that season and only escaping relegation because of the form of Walsall, Birmingham and Shrewsbury who were all effectively down by Easter.

As the transfer deadline approached, Gray made yet more changes to try and freshen up a tired looking squad. Mark Calvert was given his first team debut and Malcolm Murray was brought in from Hearts, whilst on deadline day Andy Saville was sold to Walsall for £105,000. In his place came Ian McParland from Notts County for £155,000 and a club record £200,000 was paid to Leeds United for defender Peter Swan, with Dougie Bell also coming in on loan. Paul Mudd was another 'one for the future', though his appearance in the last game of the season at Birmingham City would turn out to be his only one for the club.

In retrospect City, during Gray's season, seemed to lack mental toughness and would probably have benefited from an experienced midfield leader. Too many times they had fallen apart after going a goal down. It had been a season which had seen great changes in the playing staff and many of them would be on trial when the new season was due to start. Since the start of the 1988-89 season, Skipper, Dyer, Norman, Saville, Palmer and Hotte had left the club whilst Warren, Hesford, Whitehurst, McParland, Swan and Murray had come in with John Moore having been and gone. The team that finished the campaign was barely recognisable to the one that ended it and only Jobson, Terry and Edwards played in both the first and last games.

Though it was a terrible end to the season, there seemed at least some reasons for optimism. It was now indisputably Eddie Gray's team, we had splashed out some money and in Keith Edwards we had the highest scorer in the division.

City would undoubtedly have been in a far worse state of affairs without the goals of Keith Edwards. He could be a frustrating player but he proved to be an absolute bargain buy after Brian Horton, in one of his last transfer dealings as City's manager, signed him from Aberdeen. However, the team were too reliant on his goals. Billy Whitehurst, when he returned, did get himself on the scoresheet but Andy Saville and John Moore scored just two goals between them in 25 starts whilst Alex Dyer, Andy Payton and Ian McParland scored just seven.

However, with two or three new faces in the right areas, Edwards and Whitehurst up front, McParland to make an impact and Jobson and Swan tightening up the back, we surely had the chance of a better season? Also, the reserve team had won the championship of the Central League Second Division and some of that team, the likes of Andy Payton and Leigh Jenkinson, were pressing for a regular first team spot.

City fans were never given the chance to find out if Eddie Gray's team would improve as, on FA Cup final day, when people's thoughts were distracted by Liverpool playing Everton at Wembley, Eddie Gray and his assistant Dennis Booth were sacked. Gray had been called to see Robinson on the Friday evening to be given the news, later returning to Boothferry Park briefly to sort out personal business.

Don Robinson said at the time: '*It's a very sad day, particularly when this has to happen to people you like. It is just a matter of things not having worked out. We have taken just nine points out of the last 54 in the league and we have to look to the future of the club.*'

However, he feels now that there were other reasons why he took the decision: '*Eddie was an extremely nice person but whilst he was a great footballer, I didn't think he was the greatest motivator with people. We had, when he came, the basis of a really good team but he broke up the team with Tony Norman going to Sunderland and we lost in my mind the best goalkeeper in the league. He wanted to mould the team his way and new managers do come in and want to have a clear-out to show they are in charge in a way. With Eddie I don't think the clear out helped.*'

The news shocked many involved with City and there was sadness at such a genuinely nice man being forced out of Boothferry Park. John Cooper said: '*Eddie Gray was a dream, an absolute dream. He was a lovely man, a very professional guy in every aspect of his working day and I was very sadly disappointed that he only lasted one season.'*

Tom Wilson agreed: '*Yes, it was premature to sack him, but that was Don's outlook on life. He came up with virtually nothing from being an elevator boy in Scarborough to becoming a multi-millionaire and he couldn't stand still for a minute and he must have had it in his mind that the progress the club had made in Eddie's reign should have been quicker than it was. Eddie came, and as we know today it takes managers six to eight months to get their own team together, then they are looking forward to the first close season so they can get rid of the previous manager's players if necessary and bring in their own. Well, Eddie never got that chance and I did feel sorry for him. I can't remember where I was but he phoned me to tell me what had happened and he was devastated. He couldn't believe that he had been finished.*

'OK, we struggled and we only just managed to stay in the division, but who's to say that we might not have done better the following season once he had got his teeth into the job with the players that were there and possibly others that he would have brought in. So I don't think it was fair. Dennis finished at the same time and I came in as caretaker-manager for the second time.'

Tom was caretaker, but only during the rest of the pre-season and despite having his own backers to be made the permanent manager, it was never in his mind. He said: '*I never had ambitions to be manager. I thought I wasn't a bad coach because in my first year we had won the Premier League with the juniors which was a good achievement, and we won the reserve league a year or two later with the best goals for and against so I'd obviously done quite well in that respect. But I enjoyed the coaching side rather than the management side. I couldn't have coached players one day and sacked them the next day. I didn't have the strength of mentality to do that.*

'As caretaker I just took it as it came because I was working with the players every day anyway. These days the first team at clubs work on their own and the rest of the squad, the reserves and juniors work half a mile away. Well, at that time we all worked together and the coaches, be it Brian, Eddie, Colin to a lesser

extent and Stan worked with the team, so if there were four or five injured from the first team, the others came in and knew just what their job was, so the first team didn't play any differently from the fourth or fifth team.'

Season 1989-90

So Eddie was history and there was much speculation on who would succeed him. It didn't take long for a replacement to be named, however. Later, on the day that Gray was sacked, Robinson met up with Colin Appleton who had taken charge at Bridlington Town after unsuccessful spells in charge at Swansea and Exeter City. After about half an hour of talking, Appleton agreed to return to Boothferry Park, saying, *'I think it's nice to be able to pick up the threads at Hull City from the last time I was with them.'*

Once again, the decision was Don's and Don's alone. He explained: *'When I first became chairman I was going over to Hull three or four days a week and it was almost a full-time job but the club suffered as I got busier with my other work. With Colin Appleton, by that time I was hardly at the club, I was in France all the time so it was all done by telephone and I made the mistake there of doing something very quickly through not spending the time over in Hull. Colin had done the job before and I knew him so he was on the end of a phone, but it was one of those things that didn't work out.'*

It was the same Colin Appleton who famously told a devastated and tearful dressing room, 'Right that's it, I'm off,' just minutes after City's 1983-84 season had ended in bitter disappointment at Burnley. After leaving in such a tactless way, his was not a popular appointment, not only because of the manner of his departure last time but also because the club had moved on in his absence. We were a struggling Fourth Division club last time where the only way was up, now we were in the Second Division and desperately hoping to stay there. However, Appleton had his supporters. They could argue that he had been one of City's most successful managers, coming within one goal of taking the club from the Fourth to the Second Division in successive seasons.

Tom Wilson says of him: '*Colin was eccentric, a free spirit if you like. He had his own methods which he believed in but things change in football from week to week, as in other professions, and you have to change with them or you get left behind. When I came here in 1967 I'd been playing back four football, 4-4-2, 4-3-3 at Millwall for seven or eight years. I came here and joined Cliff Britton and it was strict man-for-man marking, the old-fashioned one, two, three and I just couldn't adapt to it, so Cliff had to change through the knowledge I'd brought from Millwall. Colin was not really prepared to change. He had his methods and he thought they should be carried out to the letter.*

There were some strange training methods but he was the manager and you had to follow it. You had to back him.

Whatever the opposing views, he had proved himself a huge success in charge of the young Tigers of the early Eighties who were looking for someone to bring on their talent, though he was to find that the dressing room in the summer of 1989 was very different. There were some grizzled older professionals who perhaps would have respected Eddie Gray for his illustrious playing career, but had not heard of Appleton and had little or no respect for him.

With Appleton back in charge of a team which had been lucky to escape relegation the season before, the close season did not engender optimism amongst supporters. The marketing of the club, unusually for Robinson, was not good. The *Hull Daily Mail* had virtually no coverage of the pre-season friendlies and a crowd of only 950 attended what should have been an attractive fixture against Hibs. Also, Mansfield Brewery announced that they were pulling out of the shirt sponsorship deal. With the announcement coming just before the new season, Robinson said, 'Obviously it is too late for us to find a new shirt sponsor for the new season so we have decided to wear the name HUMBERSIDE.' It was to prove a rare public relations disaster for the chairman as, with the overwhelming number of Hull residents favouring a return to the old East Riding of Yorkshire, most hated the name of the relatively new county.

City were the bookmakers' favourites for relegation and the first couple of months of the season saw the team do their best to live up to this billing. A creditable draw at home to Leicester was followed by defeats at Bournemouth and Grimsby, which saw us dumped out of the Littlewoods Cup. The first thirteen games of the season saw us at the bottom of the table with just eight points and no wins. Moreover, the relationship between Appleton and Keith Edwards hit rock bottom and the Golden Boot winner was first dropped and then sold to Stockport County, despite the club being desperately short of goals at the time.

One of the few players who remained in the Boothferry Park dressing room from Colin Appleton's previous time in charge was Garreth Roberts. He said: '*With Colin it was never quite the same second time around. He was good with youngsters but by that time we had all grown up and were all more experienced and he didn't get on well with some of the older players, Keith Edwards for example. It didn't go well for us but I still had great respect for him and we do meet up from time to time. He can still talk the hind legs off a donkey! Good bloke.*'

In October 1989 Colin Appleton sacked assistant Tom Wilson in what appeared to be the last throw of the dice by a man who was seen as out of his depth with experienced Second Division players.

Tom Wilson remembered: '*During that spell, we won the reserve league and the following season I joined Colin as assistant manager. After a few games of the new season, with results not going our way, he called me in one day before training. Freddie Cowell and Jeff Radcliffe were also in the room with us at the time and Colin said to me, "I'm going to have to ask you to go." I asked him, "Where to?" I thought he meant to do some scouting which we all did at the time.*

'*He said, "No, I'm going to have to ask you to go, you made a mistake last year winning that reserve league, somehow you should have lost that league because expectations of the supporters are such that they are looking for wonders to happen this season." Well talk about gobsmacked! I thought well I've heard some statements in my life both criminal and in football but I can't believe this. So from there I just came in to the dressing room, sat and wrote out a full statement in front of Jeff Radcliffe and Freddie Cowell and asked Jeff to sign it. The gist of it was that I was sacked for doing too well. Not that I'd upset him in training or hadn't done something I should have done.'*

So Tom Wilson left Boothferry Park, but it was to turn out to be a remarkably short departure and he was soon to return with Appleton going out of the door marked exit. The Brighton game was the last straw for many as City were beaten 2-0, our first ever home loss against them, and we looked certainties for relegation even so early in the season.

The Monday after the abject defeat, Don Robinson resigned. He had been away from the club for ever increasing amounts of time due to his business interests and it became clear that his mind was not on the job.

Don Robinson explained: *'I'd opened some businesses in Paris so I wasn't spending so much time at the club and was coming home on the Saturday for the match, going out again to Paris on the Monday morning and getting back by about Thursday, so I wasn't here and you can't control things that way. I was more or less conducting business on the phone from Paris and it didn't work. It was letting the club down so I stepped down.'*

The decline in the club's fortunes since Horton's sacking had become so marked that most supporters welcomed his decision, though it did mark the end of a fascinating chapter in the club's history. Tom Wilson believes that the history of Hull City will look kindly on the Don Robinson era: *'Don, in my opinion, was a great chairman for Hull City. The club was never in the red, with money always available for the manager with certain conditions attached. He was careful with the club's money and didn't spend an awful lot. He treated it as the supporter's money so everything was always done very strictly. Under Don the club did well.'*

Richard Chetham, who was related by marriage to the Needler family and was already a board member, took over as chairman although he wasn't Don Robinson's first choice. Martin Fish explains: *'Don had basically had enough when he got rid of*

LOOK BACK IN AMBER

Brian Horton and when he stepped down he asked me to be chairman. I said no because I hadn't been on the board long enough and I didn't think it was fair. Richard Chetham was on the board as Needler family representation so he became chairman.'

Chetham's first act was a popular one. He sacked Colin Appleton and installed Tom Wilson as caretaker-manager to take us through the next couple of games.

Nobody was surprised that Chetham decided on a change of manager. It was essential if the club had any hope of avoiding relegation. So the Appleton era was at an end and this intriguing figure had given his last team talk in the Boothferry Park dressing room. He is destined to be a controversial figure amongst City fans but he did play a key part in the revival of the club in the mid-1980s and came within a whisker of getting the club promoted in successive seasons.

John Cooper says of Appleton: '*Colin Appleton was very different and had a completely different aspect to how I perceive things. He was very much of the old school and he saw things in a certain way. The problem I had was the length of time he spent on the playing surface for no reason. Most managers had a plan that we agree for the training session but some of his training sessions seemed to go on and on. It was mostly the discussion on the pitch with the players rather than the application of the discussions and it was difficult for me.*

'I got on with him but he was unique in that when he'd finished his training session you would go into the dressing room and maybe see him putting boarding on the wall! He tried to turn his hand to anything. A real one-off.

It's a view that Martin Fish concurred with: '*He could mould a young side, as he had when he came in his first spell at Boothferry Park. He was experienced and had done well also at Scarborough, but the older professionals we had when he came back weren't having it. Some of the training methods were unusual and I know that Keith Edwards used to get very upset with him. I'm a believer in saying you don't try second time around, it never works.'*

NEW ERA, SAME OLD PROBLEMS

Wilson said that after being sacked by Appleton for 'being too good at his job', he had left football behind with no thoughts of a quick return: *'Within a couple of days of me leaving the club, Don had resigned and Richard Chetham took over. Richard got in touch with me at home and asked if we could meet at the ground the next day. I said no because I had been sacked and couldn't go back with Colin in charge. He told me that his plan was to sack Appleton in the morning.*

'He then invited me to meet him for lunch but again I said no, because it wouldn't have looked good, but he insisted that he would phone me the following day. He did that and said he would be sacking Colin at a specified time and invited me to come to the ground an hour later. I agreed and found out that he had indeed sacked Colin and he invited me to be the caretaker-manager again.

'So I was reinstated and thankfully the players were still in the dressing room, so he took me up there and the likes of Richard Jobson and Billy Whitehurst greeted me and said they were so pleased to see me back, which was nice.'

So Tom Wilson took the team for training but Richard Chetham's second big job - after sacking Appleton - was to appoint a new boss after Wilson made it clear he wasn't interested in taking the job on a permanent basis. Billy Bremner, some fourteen years after he had the chance to be City manager, was one of the names mentioned as a possible replacement and Ian Porterfield, Frank Stapleton and Terry Dolan were others who had their names associated with the Boothferry Park job in the week following Appleton's dismissal. But soon after a draw with Watford left us still stuck on the bottom of the table, the name Chetham had picked out of the hat was Stan Ternent. Most fans responded by asking 'Stan who?' but further research found that Ternent was the former assistant under Terry Dolan at Bradford and had been acting in a similar capacity at Crystal Palace. He had received a glowing reference from his boss Steve Coppell and was keen to try his hand at management.

Most City fans were just relieved that it was a new man in charge after the disastrous early season and looked forward to the trip to Bradford the following Saturday. We had started the year at Valley Parade in the cup under Eddie Gray and as we entered the last couple of months of 1989 we were hoping that Bradford was to be another successful away trip. Thankfully it was and a see-saw game eventually saw City leave Valley Parade with three points, their first win of the season thanks to a last minute goal by Ian McParland. City had almost forgotten how to win as their last league victory had been in March, but they had to quickly rediscover the winning habit if they were to resurrect their season.

Ternent changed the team around with Mal Shotton, Dave Bamber, Gwyn Thomas and Leigh Palin all coming into the team, but City's revival stalled with defeats coming at home to Barnsley and at Leicester before a superb Christmas programme in which the Tigers recorded four successive wins, culminating in a glorious New Year's Day victory over Sunderland at Boothferry Park.

Stan Ternent was a very different figure from Appleton and also from Eddie Gray who had gone before. Fish remembers: '*I remember Ternent saying to Richard Chetham, "If you want me to get this team successful chairman, you are going to have to spend some money." Richard went along with it and he was able to because it was his family's money, but also because he wanted success.*'

Tom Wilson, after his spell as caretaker-manager, was still on board as Ternent's assistant. He said: '*I didn't know Stan and hadn't met him before. He was an extrovert, an outgoing type and one of the best coaches I've ever worked with. He went into coaching because his playing career had finished early due to injury. He'd been at Bradford and Crystal Palace as a coach but had never been a manager and a lot of things that Stan did at Hull City were a bit naïve.*

'*He was very good at getting players to come here and he also had a fantastic financial brain on him. People tend to think that Stan ruined the club, money-wise, but he didn't. I think I saw figures fairly recently that showed that he brought in about £500,000 more than he spent. People see the outgoings that he laid out but perhaps forget the players that he sold. He would never talk to agents, who were starting to come into the game at that time. He reasoned that if players can't talk for themselves then he didn't want them.'*

John Cooper adds: '*Stan was also unique, very brash though I got on very well with him. He was totally different again to Eddie and Colin. He came to the club at a time when it was struggling big time but he had the contacts and was given some money to get the club out of that position. He was very good at begging; he smoked like a chimney and never bought a cigarette! He could cadge for the world.*

'The only argument I had with Stan was stopping him bringing his golf clubs onto the turf. He had a nine-iron which he used to try to bring on and we had many a battle, with me trying to stop him chipping a golf ball from the edge of the pitch over the East Stand! His target was the East Stand floodlight pylon.'

A week after losing 4-1 at home to Bournemouth, the Tigers fought back magnificently to win 2-1 at West Ham United, a result which took us out of the bottom three for the first time that season. Inconsistent results from then until the end of the season contained enough wins, notably away to Sunderland and home to Wolves, to ensure the club's survival and, though some of the signings did look limited and strictly short-term, they did their job in keeping the side in the division.

Season 1990-91

Another new season that began with boundless optimism. Stan Ternent performed miracles in his first season and City would have been around the play-offs if the season had started when he took over. So, it wasn't unreasonable to assume that he would provide more of the same in the new campaign. There was great hope in Ternent's ability to get the best out of the players at his disposal and Richard Chetham, the chairman, handed out details of a First Division fund to try and get the club to build on the relative success of the previous season. He assured fans that City were no longer a selling club.

LOOK BACK IN AMBER

Several more players came into the club. Russ Wilcox, David Hockaday, Tony Finnigan, David Mail and David Norton arrived but before the 1990-91 season had even begun there were problems on a pre-season tour of Bulgaria, when they lost key defender Malcolm Shotton with a hernia.

The season itself got off to a bad start with City losing at home to Notts County and then away at Blackburn. After that game, City suddenly and incredibly revoked their recently imposed no-selling policy by selling star defender Richard Jobson to Oldham Athletic, who were in the same league. Oldham had money to spend and were aiming for a promotion place, which they achieved, but the loss of Jobbo was a massive blow to the Tigers.

Tom Wilson said: '*The sale of Jobson was a big factor. Jobbo was a great player for us, defensively and offensively. He could fill in right across the back; he was a good right-back, excellent central defender and a tremendous athlete. I don't think Stan wanted him to go and the money we got for him wasn't fantastic for the calibre of player he was. He went to Oldham for a steal really and was a good servant to them over the years. Stan was looking at certain players and couldn't believe they were asking the fees they were when Jobbo was sold for that amount. We missed him.*'

However, John Cooper adds: '*I always remember I was in the directors' car park when Richard Jobson was sold. Stan said to me, "Coops, he's not as f'in good as he thinks he is." That was his way of telling me that he thought he was right to sell him on to Oldham but that was before Richard made the grade.*'

Not many City supporters would have agreed with Ternent's view of Jobson and the game after he was sold saw the Tigers at Hillsborough to face Sheffield Wednesday. Neil Buckley replaced Jobson in the centre of defence and City were awful, deservedly losing 5-1 in a shambles of a performance. City's first victory did not arrive until late September but the team did at least get two wins on the bounce to propel them towards mid-table. That was to be the best position of the season as the next game saw another hammering, 7-1 at West Ham United.

NEW ERA, SAME OLD PROBLEMS

Martin Fish said: '*The worst match in my memory was the 7-1 defeat at West Ham. I was on the board but as director, not chairman. I had to go because Richard was having a party that night and couldn't travel down to London. We got absolutely hammered and it was awful having to sit there and watch it.*'

The heavy defeats underlined how important Jobson could have been to a team which was scoring plenty of goals through the Payton/Swan partnership, but was leaking too many in at the other end with a high proportion of them being the fault of Ian Hesford. If we weren't cursing Eddie Gray for selling Tony Norman at the time, we were now. The high-scoring nature of games in the early part of the season was emphasised by a 5-2 victory over Leicester City and City needed to score four or five to be relatively sure of winning a game.

Fish explained: '*Ternent's transfers were achieving a certain amount but we were sliding down the league and Richard suddenly realised that we were spending all this money and getting nowhere. Ternent was attack-minded and defence was neglected, although he did bring Russ Wilcox in. He paid the price for results yet I still think Stan Ternent is an extremely good coach. Whether he is a good manager is difficult to say, but I saw him coaching the side and he was very good at that role. He gets a good camaraderie in the team, but it's at a price.*'

By the time of Ternent's sacking, City had scored 40 goals but had let in 63. It was obvious where the problems lay but it was not being rectified, though if the defence had been tightened up City would have been a match for most in the league.

The spirit which had characterised the escape from relegation trouble the previous season also seemed a distant memory. Garreth Roberts missed much of the season due to injury but played enough games to know what Ternent was like as a manager: '*Stan was a different type of manager completely. He was brash and I never really felt at ease with him to be honest. I always felt that he wasn't telling you everything. He was also one who bought in a lot of players for a lot of money and I didn't have respect for quite a few of them. They came in on big money and weren't particularly good players either, but he thought they were the right thing at the time. It didn't improve the dressing room.*'

LOOK BACK IN AMBER

Jeff Radcliffe was also unhappy during Ternent's reign, for the first time in his City career: '*Stan was all right sometimes but other times he would fly off the handle and you didn't know where you where with him at all, I found him very difficult. He made it awkward for me when he was at the club.*

'*I went self-employed when the club went bust and when Don took over he said he wanted me to work part-time but I could use the treatment room to do private work in the afternoon. My wages were cut by half but I could make it up through private work. So I accepted that and it went fine. I still attended all the matches, first team and reserve, but when Stan took over he wanted me to have players back at half past three, four o'clock and was wanting me to work full-time but only pay me for part-time hours.*

'*I don't think he was that good for the club as a whole. Some of the buys that Stan made were scandalous. We bought Bamber, paid his removal fees from Swindon and he bought a house in Blackpool! That showed his commitment to the club. He signed some good ones, Hockaday and Mail stand out, but then other poor signings like Finnigan from Blackburn who was a dodgy character.*

'*There were also problems in the dressing room. There was a punch-up between Stan and one of the players and Mal Shotton was trying to separate them. It's bad enough players scrapping, but when the manager gets involved you lose all respect. You've got to be big enough to walk away from it.*'

The axe came for Ternent after another humiliating away defeat, 5-1 at fellow strugglers Portsmouth. The team were bottom of the league and shipping goals at an alarming rate. City had only kept one clean sheet all season but equally, City had only failed to score in one game so there was something for the new manager to work with despite the club's perilous situation.

Ternent's sacking led to yet another spell as caretaker manager for Tom Wilson who feels that Ternent learnt a good deal during his spell in charge at Boothferry Park, which has stood him in good stead throughout his years in management:

'*Stan tried to consolidate by getting experienced players in. He did that and the following season was his learning curve. He seemed to want to do it his own way because he came to us with lots of ideas, good, bad or indifferent, from other people that he had worked with like Coppell, but he did have silly ways as well. For example he blanked the chairman, the two of them had had a row and after that he never treated his chairman with the respect that he should have done. I was acting as the go-between, I was having to take messages from Stan to the chairman and receiving messages to take back. The chairman was always trying to build a bridge and get talking again but Stan wasn't having it and it led to his downfall. The chairman was all for sacking him in the November time but I managed to talk him round and hoped that results improved over the Christmas and New Year period. But things didn't get any better either on the field or between them off the field and it came to a head, I think New Year's Day, and that was another one on his way. So I was caretaker again, I think for the fourth time.*

'I think the downfall was because the players he'd brought in, the likes of Bamber and Gwyn Thomas, their legs had gone. They had done so well the previous season but maybe didn't have it in them to continue. Stan would say that he was promised more money than he was given for certain players and the money wasn't forthcoming. I do believe that if Stan had been given more time things may have been better, I do think he would have turned it around because he was a very good coach.

'He could see things that were wrong in opposition teams and there were some players he wanted that he didn't get. The chairman, understandably, because of the broken relationship he had with Stan, just didn't want to give him any more to spend.'

A free-scoring team who could not defend to save their lives, City were two points adrift at the bottom of the Second Division and had just been humiliated 5-2 in the third round of the cup by Notts County, when Dolan arrived in the January of 1991.

Terry Dolan, as Ternent's successor, came to City from Rochdale with the Tigers having to pay the Lancashire club £40,000 in compensation. The new boss quickly bought in Jeff Lee and Bernard Ellison as his new management team and Tom Wilson went from being caretaker manager, back to his original role as reserve team boss. Dolan was greeted by a club bottom of the league, with morale low and no money to spend on new players, unlike his predecessor.

It was at this time that Martin Fish, the vice-chairman, became the chairman after Richard Chetham stood down following a heart attack. Fish explains: '*I was pleased to accept the position as a director but I never ever expected to be chairman of the club. I didn't see that at the time and we couldn't foresee the events that were going to happen, in particular Richard's heart attack. I can remember the board meeting when Richard came and said he couldn't continue because of his heart problems. The other members of the board asked who was going to take over as chairman. Richard said me and no one had a chance to speak a word, they all put their hands up and I was in, that was it.*

'*I could have said no but when Richard had his heart attack I had taken over as temporary chairman and I enjoyed the involvement, enjoyed the football and the club and everything else. The problem was I had seen that there were going to be problems in terms of financial matters.*

'*I just had to steady the ship because of all the extra expense on players. I had ambitions but I knew I had to have a manager that was not going to spend a lot of money. I could not have had another Stan Ternent for example, because we didn't have the money to do it.*

'*Also I suppose I felt I could not let the side down. If I had said no, there was nobody around that board who was going to take it on and suddenly we would have had a major problem which to the outside world would have looked even more catastrophic. So I'm not saying I was pushed into it but it was a situation where I was the accountant to try and guide us through a financially unstable time.*'

So Dolan came in to try and stop the rot and did succeed in tightening up the defence. Three loan goalkeepers were used; Kevin Dearden, Tommy Wright and Lee Butler, and David Norton was signed with Dolan also giving a chance to Leigh Jenkinson, Graham Atkinson and Lee Warren, who were not given a first team opportunity under Ternent.

The team, though it did not leap up the table, did improve in some areas and even claimed a notable scalp in defeating eventual

NEW ERA, SAME OLD PROBLEMS

champions Oldham Athletic 2-1 on the artificial pitch at Boundary Park. But the Oldham victory apart, City won only two of their remaining nine home games after Dolan took over and relegation, which had been avoided so spectacularly under Ternent the previous season, finally knocked on the Boothferry Park door.

Despite having 19 games in which to avoid relegation, Dolan's team never really looked like recovering and finished the season bottom of the table. The cold statistics were that City had won only five of those 19 games and two of those were after relegation had been confirmed. City would have been even further adrift at the bottom without the 25 goals that came from leading scorer Andy Payton.

It was ironic that the man who City had disposed of halfway through the season, Stan Ternent, was soon to show that his management career was back on track, guiding Bury to promotion from the Third Division just as Terry Dolan was leading the Tigers down into the Third to replace them. Still, whilst the jury was undoubtedly out on Terry Dolan, few blamed him for the relegation. The chairman certainly didn't and liked what he was seeing from the new man at the helm:

'Terry Dolan impressed me quite a bit because he had come from Rochdale. He had no money to work with there and they were always one of the favourites to drop out of the league, but he had got them into a top half of the table position. He had worked with no money at Rochdale and that was the position here as I was stuck with a sizeable overdraft and there were some players who probably weren't worth it from the Ternent era. Terry knew this and knew we couldn't afford to bring in any new players, he had to work with what we'd got because we couldn't increase the wage bill through increasing the numbers.

However, Tom Wilson, one of the few figures who remained at the club from Brian Horton's time, was not a fan of the new manager's coaching methods:

'I went from being assistant manager right to being on the periphery of things then, but though they were free to bring in their own people, I did feel upset about not being involved and especially about not being asked about opinions on certain players.

LOOK BACK IN AMBER

I knew the players very well but they were all new to Terry and Jeff, yet they never asked for my input.

'So Terry, Jeff and Bernard Ellison, who also came in from Rochdale, used to take training and I was left out of things. I was just a scivvy. I didn't agree with Terry's way of managing or dealing with players. He brought Jeff Lee in and in the first few sessions that I saw, I thought it was the complete opposite to what we had been doing for the last five or six years. Even as far back as the juniors and minors, we always taught them to pass the ball but Terry came in and wanted it in the opposition's half as quickly as possible and for our players to kick it as high and as long as they liked.

'He didn't encourage his players to play and it was disappointing the way it went. In the position that he took over the club, in my opinion with the players he had we could have stayed in that division comfortably. There were loads of games, loads of points to play for, but there was a kind of attitude from the management that it wasn't their team and if we went down it wasn't their fault. That was verbally mentioned quite openly and got into the mindset of the players. From that relegation the club went down and down until it nearly went out of business.'

Just before Ternent got the sack Garreth Roberts had played in what was to prove his very last game for the Tigers.

'I think it was at the Valley and I'd already had seven or eight operations on my knee and I remember turning one way and my studs caught in the ground so my knee went the other way. I remember the surgeon coming in after I'd had another operation and saying that if I carried on I would be in trouble, but the trouble was the diagnosis wasn't that clear. So there were two or three months where I was doing the wrong things, so instead of resting up and letting it heal I was playing on with it.

'In the meantime Terry Dolan had come in and he hadn't even seen me play. I remember Jeff Lee taking me into the gym at the ground where I was working really hard to get back to fitness and he said to the lads, "Look at this lad, he's really trying his guts out." So he used me as an example to the rest and I thought, "You prat." He set me up for a right mug there because all the other lads took the piss.

NEW ERA, SAME OLD PROBLEMS

'At the end of that season, I hadn't played from December onwards and we had been relegated. I was still hopeful of playing on as my contract was up at the end of that season and I was worried about what I was going to do next. Terry got me in the office and offered me the job of youth team manager and made Jeff Radcliffe come into the room and tell me that my knee wasn't looking good.

'I felt that he was twisting Jeff's arm to say that I was finished. So it was a case of finish playing and go into the managerial side. I'd lost my driving licence at this time so I wasn't driving and I told him this but I thought it wouldn't have had any impact on the job.

'I'd been given the weekend to think about it because it was a big step facing up to not playing again and going into another role. I went in on the Monday and said that yes, I'd love to do it. He turned round to me and said, "Sorry I've changed my mind; I've taken the job away from you now." So with that I went ballistic and stormed out. He'd used the thing about me losing my licence as an excuse not to employ me, saying that he'd be wanting me to drive the minibus. So I thought if they didn't want me for my coaching, and the passion, enthusiasm and knowledge, and all they really wanted was a bus driver, then fine, they could shove it.

'Mal Shotton got the job and he had a year of his contract to go so they sussed that they'd have to give me another contract whereas it wouldn't have cost them anything to employ Mally in that job. That left a really bitter taste because a lot of the guys I'd been around at the start, Ken Houghton and Chris Chilton, were legends at the club and had been at the club as youth team manager. By this time I'd played 490-odd games and I thought I deserved an opportunity as well because I'd had numerous opportunities to move away from the club during my time but never took them. So it was a kick in the teeth.'

PART FIVE

The Dolan years

Season 1991-92

City were lucky to have Andy Payton still with the club after relegation but after his success the previous season, it was only a matter of time before he left with a number of clubs reportedly interested in signing him. Ian Hesford, Peter Swan, Ian McParland and Tony Finnigan had all left the club with only new goalkeeper Alan Fettis being signed before the new season.

City got off to a good start, winning 1-0 at Reading, and whilst Payton stayed it appeared there may be a chance of the play-offs. City beat Shrewsbury 4-0 on Bonfire Night and Chester at home the following Saturday, by which time Payton had scored six goals in five games to send City up to eighth in the table. However, it was the last contribution that the forward made in a Tigers shirt as he was sold to Middlesbrough for £750,000 to leave the club desperately short of strikers.

Dolan could not look to the boardroom for any money to replace Payton as the £750,000 was spent paying off debts. Martin Fish was finding it hard to make the sums add up with gates so low. He had his own plans for the club but was frustrated in his attempts to boost the club's fortunes.

He said: '*We had had a change of bank manager and it wasn't the best change in the world. Also, I could see things tightening up generally in football and we were not in a good position because Richard had spent a lot of money, it had all gone and there were overdrafts. So I could see we were going to have to be very careful and initially it was going to be quite an austere type of existence.*

'*I was hoping to do more with the ground. I announced that we would be going to have a new East Stand and I had spent a lot of time in London getting a million pound grant for it. It was going to cost us only £200,000 for a 6,000 all-seater stand on that side and I thought that was money well spent as it would start to improve the ground, but at the same time, Christopher Needler announced that the Needler family was going to pull out of Hull City so we never got any further.*'

The loss of Payton on the field was apparent the next time the team took to the field at Morecambe in the first round of the FA Cup.

LOOK BACK IN AMBER

City fans had to contend with the sight of Herry Ngata and Neil Buckley as our strikers! It was a going to be a long afternoon and though we beat them 1-0 it was not an impressive victory and the sight of Buckley upfront stayed with City fans for a long time afterwards.

Dolan tried to improve his side by signing Imre Varadi, a player who hardly endeared himself to City fans by reportedly saying that the Tigers were the last team he would play for. However, there was no doubt that we needed a forward so an appeal was launched for the £50,000 needed to bring the 33-year-old striker to Boothferry Park. Within a week the total had reached over £36,000 which included £10,000, the sum raised by the 'Put a Tiger in Your Team' cash fund.

So, it had come to this. So soon after being a progressive club in the Second Division, City were becoming a small fish in the lower leagues, having to scratch around for small change to buy a has-been striker who never wanted to come to City in the first place.

After the Morecambe defeat, City won at Blackpool to set up an FA Cup third round tie at home to Chelsea but, frustratingly, with the biggest crowd at Boothferry Park for years, the Tigers tried to outpass their opponents and predictably failed, losing the tie 2-0.

Despite the FA Cup victories, City had not won in the league since the sale of Andy Payton and went 11 games before winning 1-0 away at Darlington, by which time City had fallen into the bottom four. However victories over Huddersfield, leaders Stoke and Shrewsbury gave the Tigers some respite in what was turning into a relegation battle. Defeats against Bury and Brentford sent City hurtling back towards the relegation zone but four wins to end the season with saw City safe from the drop. The summer saw free transfers given to Nicky Brown, Malcolm Shotton, Neil Buckley, Ken De Mange and Herry Ngata.

Playwright Alan Plater joining the Tigers for training in the
early 1970s. Those pointing the finger at Plater are, from the
left, Tommy Cavanagh, Roger DeVries, Ian Butler, Jeff
Wealands, Phil Holme, Terry Neill, Ken Wagstaff, Ken
Houghton, Malcolm Lord, Frank Banks and Andy Davidson.

Fashion guru Stuart Pearson joins team-mates Malcolm Lord
and Ken Wagstaff to play a round of golf.

Stuart 'Pancho' Pearson, through on goal against West Ham United in the FA Cup, 1973.

John Kaye leads out the Tigers for the Watney Cup against Stoke City in August 1973. Jimmy Greenhoff leads out Stoke and within a year, he and Pearson would be team-mates at Old Trafford, Pearson joining Manchester United for £200,000.

City ready for take-off at the start of the 1974-75 season. Among those in the photograph are Wilf Dixon, Jeff Radcliffe, Jeff Hemmerman, John Hawley, Roy Greenwood, Stuart Blampey, Roger DeVries, Terry Neill, Jeff Wealands, Steve Deere, Vince Grimes and, at the end in the stripy blazer, Ken Wagstaff. Neill was soon to leave the Tigers to take up the manager's job at Spurs.

John Kaye and his team prepare for an away game during the 1974-75 season. From the left, Kaye, McGill, Davidson, Hemmerman, Galvin, Daniel, Wealands, Deere, Hawley, Banks and Wood. Malcolm Lord is on the coach step.

The City squad at the start of the 1977-78 season. Paul Haigh
is sat down and among others captured are Jeff Radcliffe,
John Hawley, Gordon Nisbet, Roger DeVries, Billy Bremner,
George Lyall, Malcolm Lord, John Kaye, Bruce Bannister,
Peter Daniel, Bobby Collins and Ian Dobson.

John Kaye with the board of directors and two new recruits
at the start of the 1977-78 season, Bobby Collins (second from
the right) and Bruce Bannister. Bob Chapman and
Christopher Needler are in the centre of the photograph.

City players in pre-season training in the late 1970s. Roger DeVries, Eddie Blackburn and Keith Edwards are among those shown.

The North Stand at Boothferry Park. When the team slid down the leagues, the plan for a huge new development on the site was scrapped and the stand was replaced by a supermarket and a small open terrace.

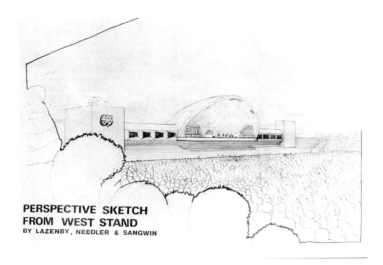

PERSPECTIVE SKETCH FROM WEST STAND
BY LAZENBY, NEEDLER & SANGWIN

Above: When Don Robinson took over, he planned to build a 'Hollywood Dome' on top of the North terrace which would attract top rock bands to play in the city.
The plan was quietly shelved.
Below: The East Stand at Boothferry Park was a site awaiting development since City won promotion to the Second Division in 1985. This was one plan to build a two-tier stand to seat 5,000.

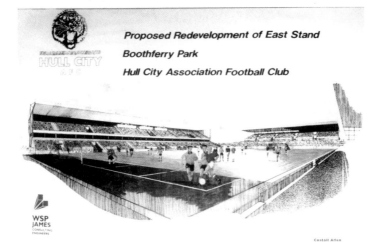

Proposed Redevelopment of East Stand

Boothferry Park

Hull City Association Football Club

The City team at the start of the 1980-81 season, with
established players such as Haigh, Nisbet and Horswill joined
by Garreth Roberts, Brian Marwood and Steve McClaren,
players who would guide the club back up the leagues.

The first step to playing on the Moon. This was one of Don
Robinson's early trips abroad, to Calella in Spain.

Ken Houghton, Wilf McGuinness and Jeff Radcliffe among those turning out for City in a pre-season game in Holland in 1979.

The newly-suited Tigers at the start of the 1982-83 season. The new management team of Colin Appleton and Chris Chilton would guide the club to promotion from the Fourth Division.

The Tigers strike at the heart of what was later to become
Malcolm Glazer territory with the 'British Invasion', another
of Don Robinson's schemes to get the Tigers noticed.
This picture sees the City squad, complete with bowlers and
brollies, strolling down the Main Street in Disneyland Florida.

This is the poster
advertising the City game
against the Tampa Bay
Rowdies at the Tampa
Stadium.

Garreth Roberts leads the Tigers out at Boothferry Park during the 1984-85 promotion season.

Indisputably City's most embarrasing sponsorship deal. While others had EMI, Sharp and Phillips on their shirts, the Tigers had Twydale Turkeys!

Tigers reunited. Some ex-Tigers come back to Boothferry Park for Garreth Roberts' testimonial game. Back row left to right; Gary Swann, Leigh Jenkinson, Stan McEwan, Brian Horton, Ian Hesford, Billy Whitehurst, Peter Skipper, Pat Heard, Keith Edwards. Front row; Andy Payton, Garreth Roberts, Dennis Booth, Graeme Atkinson, Steve McClaren and Billy Askew.

A packed South Stand at Boothferry Park. When the Kempton declined in the Eighties and Nineties, most of the 'Boothferry roar' was confined to the former Bunkers Hill.

Peter Swan is amongst those clearing snow from the Boothferry Park pitch during the 1990-91 season.

Fireworks light up Boothferry Park on Bonfire Night 1991 before City played Shrewsbury.

Another day, another saviour. Tom Belton rides to the rescue after David Lloyd sells the club to the Buchanan/Hinchcliffe consortium.

Justin Whittle, Jon Schofield and Lee Bracey are among those lining up before City played Guiseley in a pre-season friendly at the beginning of the 1999-2000 season.

John Cooper has come through the Needler, Fish, Lloyd and Buchanan times and still lives to tell the tale. He still works as Stadium Manager at the KC.

Brian Little, still a hero to many at Hull City for the way he kept the team going through the lock-outs and administration.

Gary Brabin, one of the figureheads of the 'great escape' season. Many thought Little made a big mistake by releasing him after the 2000-2001 season.

The Hull City nameplate, or rather the plastic replica, after the original was controversially sold by Martin Fish.

The latter day Boothferry Park experience. When the Kempton was re-opened during the Buchanan years, the atmosphere at the ground received a huge boost and the East Stand was regularly sold out. This is the entrance to the Kempton with the visitors' entrance on the extreme right.

Action from the last ever competitive game at
Boothferry Park, a 1-0 defeat against Darlington.
A typically botched farewell.

City fans on the pitch after the Darlington game, saying their
own goodbyes to Boothferry Park.

Season 1992-93

The Tigers started the 1992-93 season looking more like tigers than ever before. Martin Fish and Terry Dolan combined to design a kit which certainly stood out though it attracted a fair amount of ridicule throughout the football world.

On the pitch, the 'Put a Tiger in your team' campaign had raised over £11,000 and though it did not attract Imre Varadi to Boothferry Park a year earlier, it did enable the club to bring in Linton Brown, who was picked up from non-league where he had played for Bridlington, North Ferriby and Guiseley. Before Brown's arrival, over the past couple of years City had brought in John Pearson, Tony Kelly and Gary Lund on loan with a view to signing them permanently, but the club had been unable to afford them, so Dolan turned to the 24-year-old who had scored 16 goals in 20 games for Guiseley.

The club had been looking for a goalscorer since Andy Payton had left and whereas Pearson had been a target man, Brown was more of a Payton substitute, using his speed to get himself into goalscoring positions. He was also among some familiar faces as he had, at various times, played alongside Dean Windass, Darren France and Gary Hobson in non-league and joined other Hull-born players in the squad at the time, notably Graeme Atkinson, Neil Allison, Steve Wilson, Stuart Young and Matty Edeson.

The young squad looked to Norton, Mail and Hockaday for experience and had a setback before the season with the refusal of Russ Wilcox to sign a new contract. This meant that Gary Hobson and Neil Allison, two youngsters, had the chance to form a new central defensive partnership whilst Dolan was looking for more from the likes of Windass, Graeme Atkinson, Leigh Jenkinson and Paul Hunter for goals. He brought in Gary Lund before the first game of the season to add more options upfront.

Despite beating promotion favourites Stoke in the first game of the season, it was another struggle with City always closer to the bottom than the top of the table. However, it started off well. City drew with Chester, beat Plymouth at home with Peter Shilton sent off, and further victories over Swansea and Reading saw City second in the table after five games.

City then went 11 games without a win, losing at home to Bradford and Huddersfield before getting a win, beating Darlington away as they had done the season before, to halt a dreadful run which left City near the relegation zone.

City's last home game of the season saw City three points ahead of the fourth bottom Preston, with promotion-chasing Bolton coming to Boothferry Park. There was anger amongst supporters, though aimed mainly at the police rather than the club, when City fans were told that they would not be allowed in the East Stand for the game as it was needed to accommodate the away fans who were expected to travel over.

If ever the club felt small-time it was now. Many City fans could see the sense in the decision as the North Terrace held barely 1,500, the East Stand about the same and with City's crowds being low at the time, the South Stand could comfortably hold all the home support. However, it was the impression that it gave out to other clubs. We were small-time not in the same bracket as Bolton and it worried those of us who still held out hopes of a return to the Second Division. What would happen when Leeds, Sunderland, Sheffield United and other teams with a big away following came to Boothferry Park?

It was to be a horrible night as Bolton won the game 2-1 scoring the winner three minutes from time. The goal sparked a pitch invasion from their fans with City defender Rob Miller knocked to the ground and then kicked by their fans.

The traumatic game meant that City were not mathematically certain of safety going into the last game of the season away to West Brom. We lost the game but results elsewhere saw us safe and Preston were relegated. However, it was a poor campaign and left fans with little to look forward to unless there was to be a major injection of money. An unlikely prospect.

Off the field, Tom Wilson was suddenly relieved of his coaching duties but was offered the position of club secretary, a job he was happy to accept. '*I jumped at the chance to be secretary because I could put my administrative skills to good use. I had been in Law for many years so could organise things and I obviously wasn't going to get any more work on the training field, so it was the next best thing. I still used to travel with the team; I used to take my secretary's work with me on the journeys and occasionally the players used to come and sit with me.*

'I'd been with these players for quite a few years by then so they used to sit with me and I could see that Terry and Jeff were uncomfortable with that. I used to talk to the lads about the game and they used to moan to me about the orders to play it high and long. I used to say to the players that I may not agree with it but the manager picks the team. I think Terry believed that I may be saying things that I shouldn't have been saying but I would not have done that.'

Wilson maintains that whatever his own doubts about the management duo of Dolan and Lee, he never criticised them when talking to the players, even when the players came to him with their own criticisms of the tactics and coaching.

He goes on: '*Sadly it got to the stage where he stopped the players coming over to my office at the front. I never said anything derogatory to the players because it wasn't my place to. I felt it inwardly and spoke to some of the ex-players like Ken Houghton, but not to the players. One example was when Gary Hobson came across to my office almost in tears. In my opinion Gary Hobson and Neil Allison should have been the backbone of Hull City for ten years. They were both good central defenders and were good footballers who knew when to play it long and knew when to pass it. But both of them had been told just to get rid, to get it up there, out of the way.*

'I was saying to Gary that whilst I may agree with him, I had no say in tactics anymore and of course at that moment Terry Dolan walked in without even knocking, so straight away I changed the subject and said something like, "I think you should see the PFA about that," we started talking about pensions. I wasn't worried about me, I was worried about Gary getting into trouble and from that day on the lads were stopped from coming across to see me. I was also banned from the team coach which broke my heart because I'd been at Hull City a

*long time at that point and felt part of the club. The excuse from
the chairman was that he didn't want any non-football people
on the coach and yet Simon Cawkhill, the commercial manager
who knew nothing about football at all, was still allowed to
travel on the coach.'*

Wilson nevertheless threw himself into his new job, enjoying
the chance to put his administration skills to the test. He was also
desperately keen to help improve the club's fortunes off the field.
With the club losing so much money every week, he was sure that
any schemes he could assist with would be gratefully accepted by
the chairman. However, it did not work out that way. He says: '*I
was always looking at ways of making money for the club. I did
research on catering, for example. We had a little tea hut on the
East Stand, I think there was one under the West Stand and if you
went for a cup of tea at half-time you were probably down there for
20 minutes queuing. I went to Sheffield United, Notts Forest,
Sheffield Wednesday and worked with their secretaries and looked
at their catering arrangements for matchdays. I got all these
figures, put them together and put them to Mr Fish and he just poo-
pooed them. So instead of making money, we were paying £12-
£13,000 a year for a chap to come over all the way from
Nottingham to run these two team huts, so we were paying out
money for someone to run it rather than us running it ourselves and
making money.*

'*We also had the gymnasium which was hardly being used and
I had got in touch with East Riding Council and the chief executive
came to see me. I took him across to see it and he couldn't believe
that there was such a building in the north-east of England not
being used. We had quite a few meetings together which the
chairman knew about.*

'*The council were willing to come and refurbish the whole
gymnasium to break it down into international-sized tennis courts
with seating at the side. We could have had international basketball
or badminton and we were going to make it into a sports centre
with seating. We would put in a bar, a refreshment area, new
dressing rooms, showers etc, and that was all going to be Hull
City's between 9am and about 1.30pm every day.*

'There were also plans to resurface all the back pitches and make them all-weather and that would also not cost the club a penny. So it would be ours every day until after 1pm and the rest of the time it would be used as a sports centre. The nearest one was Haltemprice at that time so the attraction was there. It was a wonderful project which would really benefit the club but the chairman wouldn't even meet the executive.

'He said there must be a trick in it and they would want something out of it. I said that they didn't and pleaded with him to at least meet them to discuss it. It was a way of the club making money and it badly needed it. They were going to pay us rather than us paying them but he wouldn't even meet them to discuss it. I couldn't believe it but I kept on trying to make money for the club because it was becoming difficult to meet the wages every week.'

Season 1993-94

The previous two campaigns had seen the club struggle at the wrong end of the Second Division table and hopes, at least among supporters, were not high. Russ Wilcox finally got his move away from Boothferry Park, opting to further his career by moving to Doncaster, whilst David Norton was anxious to follow him out, saying amusingly, 'I'm ready to tackle the Premier League.'

The feeling amongst the bookmakers was that City were among the favourites for the drop along with Exeter and Hartlepool, but the first game of the season saw City beat Barnet 2-1 away from home with a side of Wilson, Mitchell, Hobson, Warren, Allison, Abbot, Norton, Moran, Brown, Windass and Atkinson. Windass was only playing up front because of a shortage of strikers with both Chris Hargreaves and Steve Moran on the treatment table, leaving Dolan with the decision to begin the campaign with Windass and Brown up front.

Whether managerial masterstroke or lucky break, it led to a fantastic start to the season with City getting to the top of the table with memorable performances against Cambridge and Cardiff away, with both games finishing 4-3 to the Tigers, Windass scoring a hat-trick in the first of those games. One game that sticks in my memory was the Coca-Cola Cup first round second leg game against Notts County. We were 2-0 down from the first leg and there were only around 2,000 at Boothferry Park to see the return game, but City produced probably the best performance under Dolan that I witnessed, deservedly winning the game 3-1, only losing out on the away goals rule.

Another memorable performance in the early part of the season was a 1-0 victory over Brentford in which City had to play part of the game with nine men as referee Brian Coddington sent off City's two full-backs, Brian Mitchell and Gary Hobson, as well as booking six others. To add to his popularity with City fans he refused to allow Jeff Radcliffe to come onto the field to attend to a head injury to Mitchell before he was sent off.

By mid-September, a month into the new season, City were top of the Second Division playing some wonderful attacking football with the new partnership of Windass and Linton Brown making the most of the headlines. At this stage of the season City were the only team to have a 100% away record, 16 points out of a possible 18, the country's leading scorer in Windass who had scored eight, and were the Second Division's leading scorers with 16 in total.

Windass was the catalyst for the revival. Rejected by Horton for being too small, he was brought back to the club from North Ferriby and was a huge success almost immediately. Martin Fish remains a fan of the player: '*My favourite players were Windass and Brown when he was on song. The speed of Brown and the link with Windass was great to see. We gave Windass a lot of help and rescued him in a way. If you talk to Dean Windass he'll talk of Terry Dolan and myself in very favourable terms because he felt as though he was going on the scrapheap and was rescued from it. We had to help him in a lot of ways.*'

However, City were not a one-man team. Linton Brown was in the form of his life and in Hobson and Allison, City had two defenders who looked to have a big future in the game. City were trying to boost their good start to the season with action in the transfer market and the media reported that City had put in a bid of

£200,000 for Martin Carruthers, who had looked good the previous season when he came to City on a three-month loan. To those who raised eyebrows as the club had pleaded poverty for years, Dolan explained that at the time he put in the bid, he knew that he would be receiving £200,000 from Coventry City for Leigh Jenkinson. However, Carruthers did not return to the Tigers and before the start of the 1993-94 season he joined Stoke City from Aston Villa for £300,000.

Perhaps this was the time to speculate to accumulate; the best start in years had crowds up, if only a little, but the financial problems for the club remained.

John Cooper said: '*Martin was very good with his administration but he came at a time when funding was the most important thing and the funding simply wasn't available to him. Had Martin had the money, Boothferry Park would have been upgraded and I believe that year, around 1994 or 95, Terry Dolan had the makings of quite a good side. It was just when it needed that final push, post-Christmas, when funding should have been made available. It never was.*'

Meanwhile, Tom Wilson was beginning to get the distinct feeling that he was being sidelined. Though there may not have been a deliberate plan to ostracise him, that was what was happening:

'*Even in the boardrooms it was getting embarrassing. The manager and coach would come up after a game and the chairman would join them so the three of them had a clique and I was left on my own. I didn't feel that was right but I was never upset enough to do anything about it. It just made me feel sad because it wasn't as if the two of them were taking us up a division and we were flying high. The club was going down fast and, looking at it from a professional and a realistic point of view, it was definitely going towards extinction and yet they couldn't see it. They couldn't see the wood for the trees or perhaps didn't want to.*

'*I never had a physical or verbal falling out with Terry Dolan or Jeff Lee; I was always polite to them, in fairness they were always polite to me to my face but what was going on behind the scenes I wasn't too sure about.*'

LOOK BACK IN AMBER

The funding crisis at the club was used as the reason to finally dispense with the services of Wilson. He had been associated with the club in one way or another for 27 years but was sacked from his position as secretary in what was claimed to be a cost-cutting measure. The Scot revealed afterwards that he had offered to take a pay cut to stay on the payroll and said that in his opinion Martin Fish hardly gave the matter any consideration, which was even more hurtful.

He remembers: '*Martin used to come into my office once or twice a week. I think a Thursday was when we used to go through the club's finances or any other business, so he just came in one day and sat down as normal. He said to me, "Oh, I've got a letter for you," so I said, "Oh thanks very much," and put it to one side. He said "No, I'd rather that you read it now." I said I had a lot of other business to get through, but he insisted that he wanted me to read it immediately so I opened it and it said I had been made redundant. We are dispensing with your services forthwith etc.*

'*I asked him what was going on and he said that he was going to have to ask me to go. So I just stood up and told him I was going to see my solicitor. He said that he didn't want me to go immediately but I put my jacket on, got my briefcase and went. And I did go straight to my solicitor, who couldn't believe it. He couldn't believe that the chairman had handled it in that way. I could have taken the club for a lot of money but again, I didn't feel it was right. I'm a supporter, I love the club and there's no way I could have done that.*

'*The way it was done was just laughable. A schoolchild wouldn't have handled it the way that Martin Fish did and it was nothing to do with finance. There were a lot of financial situations that I was trying to rectify for the club at the time. Jeff Lee and Bernard Ellison were travelling in every day from the other side of Bradford and getting petrol money but the figures for their petrol monthly were unbelievable. They were never asked to come and live in Hull or if they were I didn't hear it. At least Terry Dolan came to live in Ferriby. I just thought it was wrong and it was part of my job as secretary to bring that to the attention of the chairman, but these matters were always discarded and always being pushed to one side.*

THE DOLAN YEARS

'So he took over the role himself, which was laughable in the eyes of other clubs and for me it was heartbreaking to leave the club after all that time.'

Thankfully, Wilson was not lost to football: '*I'm fortunate enough that when I left Hull City one of the first people to get in touch with me was Brian Horton, who wanted me to do some coaching for him. I think he was at Oxford then. Then again, whilst he was at Manchester City he offered me a coaching position but I said no. I thought I had had my time coaching. I was doing some scouting for them once or twice a week and kept in touch with the game that way'.*

At the time of Wilson's departure, the Tigers were still high up the Second Division table with Bradford City due to visit Boothferry Park. It was a timely visit as City were in financial trouble again; the club had been told to pay a VAT bill of £30,000 by the Tuesday after the game or face a High Court appearance later in the week. Fish was confident that the gate receipts from the Bradford game would stave off the threat and went public on his hope for a big gate.

The club got their wish as the crowd of 9,492 was the highest league gate at Boothferry Park since Dolan took charge of the team. It also produced gate receipts healthy enough to ward off the Inland Revenue, at least for the time being. Not only that but the Tigers produced a performance to match. Everything went perfectly with City dominating from the start and taking the lead through Dean Windass after just five minutes. A clearly pumped-up Deano didn't last long on the field though, as just four minutes later the referee, a young and inexperienced Jeff Winter, prepared to take Deano's name, Windass gave the referee a mouthful and was sent off, leaving City having to defend the lead for another 81 minutes.

Sean McCarthy soon equalised for Bradford, getting himself a booking for goading the South Stand as part of his celebrations, but though Bradford were getting the upper hand, City showed great spirit to take a hold of the game. With Linton Brown playing the role of a lone striker to perfection, keeping their defence busy all afternoon, City took control with Greg Abbot scoring a first half penalty and Linton himself getting the winner. The 3-1 win put City back on top of the table.

LOOK BACK IN AMBER

The excellent start to the season added to the opinion that in Dolan and Lee, City had a management duo that could lead the club back into what was now known as the First Division. They had the respect of the fans and any complaints about negative football and long-ball tactics were quietened as the team went on the best run for several years. It was a time that Martin Fish remembers fondly:

'Terry was fair but firm with the players, he was a bit of a disciplinarian, not an especially tough one but the players knew where they stood with him and he developed a dressing room which really did have camaraderie amongst them. There was tremendous team spirit with the likes of Dean Windass, Linton Brown and David Norton, and others who jollied everyone up, which did an awful lot for morale.

'Jeff Lee was a tough character, but Terry had the measure of players and never let them get away with anything. So I was impressed and I feel he did a decent job for me, even if others didn't think so.'

Being top of the table didn't last long, however, as a run of four defeats in five league games set City back, but there were enough victories; notably 4-1 at home to Rotherham and 2-0 away at Bournemouth to leave the supporters still hoping for the play-offs at least. It's tempting to think that if the financial situation of the club had been healthier, City might have been able to sustain a more effective promotion challenge that season but it was not to be, and City were making headlines as much for their debt as for the success on the pitch.

Christopher Needler entered the controversy into the financial crisis at the club by revealing that he would sell the club for £1 if any buyer was willing to put up £750,000 in cash. After two takeover bids failed, he effectively changed his mind, saying that he would now only hand over control to Martin Fish because of the 'time and commitment' that the chairman had put into the club. He added that the club had nearly been forced to close before selling Andy Payton to Middlesbrough and said that the financial problems had been caused by the club spending too much money on players in the past without ensuring that gate receipts would cover wages and loyalty bonuses.

THE DOLAN YEARS

Though the Bradford game staved off the threat of High Court action, it was only a temporary stay of execution as later in the season, as the debts continued to pile up, City were sent to the High Court due to another outstanding bill of £220,000 owed to the Inland Revenue. It led to Martin Fish again appealing to the businesses of Hull to support the club and he stressed how important it was to get more fans to Boothferry Park. He stated:

'Hull City in its present situation cannot run on the crowds we have been getting. With success we need something between 7 and 8 thousand, which would bring us profit.'

The appeal to local businesses partly worked as £180,000 was raised to enable the winding-up order to be staved off for another month. However, as the club prepared for the High Court return, a home victory over Exeter, hardly the biggest draw, brought a crowd of just over 4,500 to Boothferry Park which, once again, brought a warning from Mr Fish. He issued a 'support your club or we may be forced to sell players' call, warning that the club could not survive on such attendances, though he was confident that the further money needed to ward off the Inland Revenue could be raised.

On the field City still had the play-offs in mind, but despite the start we made, it was always in hope rather than expectation. The squad wasn't strong enough and we were relying too heavily on the Windass and Brown partnership to keep the club towards the top. As the season entered its latter stages, Dolan brought in reinforcements in the shape of Simon Dakin, who was signed from Derby reserves, and Garreth Williams from Barnsley, but a disappointing 3-1 defeat at Turf Moor towards the end of March just about signalled the end of City's hopes of appearing in the play-offs and led to Lee Warren playing his last game for the club.

The midfielder, who, having been one of Eddie Gray's signings, was the longest-serving player at the club, had been instrumental in City's good season but in the Burnley game he was substituted about 10 minutes after himself coming on as a sub for David Mail. Dolan blamed him for all three goals, hence his decision to replace him, but it infuriated the defender who threw his shirt at the manager as he stormed down the tunnel.

LOOK BACK IN AMBER

Soon after, with the club already resigned to another season in the Second Division, the manager announced his retained list early, waving goodbye to Warren and Rob Miller. Most supporters felt that Warren had done more than enough to earn a new contract, but Dolan disagreed, saying:

'Without going into too much detail and bearing in mind a lot of the circumstances which I don't want to go into in public, we had a talk and both felt it could be time for him to have a change and a fresh start.'

The close season began with City's future still uncertain due to the Inland Revenue debt, but it was also dominated, at least in the first couple of weeks, by the future of Terry Dolan. There was a managerial vacancy at Valley Parade, home of Bradford City, where Dolan had previously been manager and Martin Fish confirmed that he had been in discussions with his counterpart at Bradford, Geoffrey Richmond, and though the two clubs were in the same division, there were obvious attractions for Dolan.

He was familiar with the club and it was also apparent that the two clubs at that time were moving in different directions. In the same week as the news broke, Martin Fish delivered an end of season message saying that there would be no money for new players and none forthcoming in the foreseeable future. Maybe not the sort of news to persuade the missing thousands back to Boothferry Park and, by contrast, Richmond, who had moved to Bradford from being chairman of Scarborough, had money to spend and was making ambitious plans for the club's future. The news of Dolan's possible departure lasted for another week before the news came through that he was to stay as manager of City, though it was not clear whether or not he had been interviewed for the Bradford job.

On the playing side, the club were resigned to losing the services of David Norton who again turned down the offer of a new contract. He had been offered the same terms as the season before but held out for more and it appeared that he had played his last game in a City shirt when he finally secured a move away from Boothferry Park, joining Northampton on a month's loan at the start of the new season.

Season 1994-95

The 1994-95 season saw the East Stand, which had had a severely reduced capacity for the last decade, threatened with complete closure. It was to be closed for the Coca-Cola Cup tie against Scarborough and Martin Fish warned that, though it would reopen after crush barriers were installed, the Football Licensing Authority were looking to close it completely from the beginning of the 1995-96 season.

There was little transfer news with the only new arrivals in the close season being Craig Lawford and Jimmy Graham, both who came with strong Bradford connections. As the season got underway chairman Martin Fish warned that despite the team doing well in the previous season, gates were still too low with the club needing attendances of about 6,000 to break even.

City got off to a terrible start, losing at Oxford 4-0 on the opening day and losing their first home league game of the season, 2-0 to Swansea. City also went out of the Auto Windscreen Cup with a 2-0 home defeat to Doncaster in front of only 890 fans, but performances soon took a turn for the better as the Windass and Linton Brown partnership up front once again began to bear fruit. An eight match unbeaten run was launched at St Andrews where City came away with a two-all draw despite being down to ten men for some of the game. Greg Abbot was sent off for letting one of their players punch him, or that's how it looked from where City fans were stood.

In October, in the middle of a good run of form, much of Hull was in mourning as the death was announced of Raich Carter, one of the city's true footballing legends, who had done so much to transform football in the city post-war. His funeral cortege passed Boothferry Park and all the playing and non-playing staff stood outside, heads bowed in respect. The following Saturday City played at home to Crewe and after a perfectly respected minute's silence, the Tigers ran out 7-1 winners with Linton Brown scoring a hat-trick.

LOOK BACK IN AMBER

Further wins over York and Brentford saw us up to fourth in the table and we were confident of progress in the FA Cup against Third Division Lincoln City. Despite City doing little wrong in the league we were appalling against Lincoln showing none of the good football which we had played for most of the season. Our tactics appeared to be solely to hoof the ball upfield for our forwards to chase, something which was to become a familiar moan over the next few years but which didn't work in this game as Lincoln came away with a 1-0 win and a place in the Second Round.

City were out of the cup but their league form didn't suffer too badly and they were fifth in the table when Oxford came to Boothferry Park the week before Christmas. City were badly hit by injuries and were forced into naming Alan Fettis as an outfield substitute despite bringing in Ray Wallace and Paul Cox as new loan signings. Oxford opened the scoring that day but Windass scored twice for City before Fettis came on up front towards the end of the game. Most thought he would be sent on to shore up the defence to try and secure the points, but Fettis, though he showed little else in his display, stayed upfield and towards the end of the game, in a goalmouth scramble, managed to shoot home to put City 3-1 up against one of their promotion rivals and send Boothferry Park wild.

On Boxing Day Huddersfield Town were the visitors to Hull and a crowd of over 10,000, such a rarity in the 1990s, were present including a couple of thousand from West Yorkshire with their team pushing for promotion. It was a pulsating game, probably more for the atmosphere than on the field action, and most seemed to think that City had got away with it when Uriah Rennie, new to the referees' list, denied Town what appeared to be a blatant penalty in front of the South Stand, but we nevertheless looked the better team and were rewarded towards the end of the game when Richard Peacock scored a wonderful goal to send us home happy.

A couple of days later, City fans turned up in numbers at Valley Parade, Bradford, to see if City could consolidate their position towards the top of the table, but a late winner from John Taylor left us defeated, though we were still well placed in the play-off zone.

THE DOLAN YEARS

In the second half of the season, City's lack of resources and small squad numbers again began to have an effect, much as it appeared to do the season before. City were becoming too inconsistent to challenge for promotion, though Dolan tried to improve the squad with loan signings coming in the shape of Warren Joyce and Ian Ormondroyd. Both made some impact - Ormondroyd scored on his City debut as Cardiff were beaten 4-0 - though some fans saw his signing as a way of justifying the long-ball game that most fans despised.

One game stood out for the wrong reasons. Birmingham City, top of the table, came to Boothferry in front of just short of 10,000 and came away with a point, though they had a less than comfortable journey back to the West Midlands after an attack on the team bus which resulted in several broken windows and a slight injury to manager Barry Fry. It portrayed City in a terrible light and Martin Fish won praise for vowing to ban for life anyone who was found guilty of involvement in the offence.

As the season drew to a close and the play-offs became more and more unlikely, some signs of dissatisfaction with the management team began to emerge. A 3-1 defeat away to York was particularly memorable for a rotten performance and some in the big City following spending much of the game loudly criticising Dolan from the terraces.

Management and supporters were soon reunited though and both were critical of referee David Orr during our game away to Brighton. We desperately needed the win to get into the play-off places and looked to have the goal we needed when a Gary Lund header was fumbled over the line by their keeper. It was already a couple of feet over the line before the keeper clawed it back again, bundling over Rob Dewhurst in the process in a scene reminiscent of that by former City keeper Roy Carroll for Manchester United in 2005.

The linesman signalled that the ball had crossed the line and the referee rightly awarded the goal. However, as City players and fans celebrated and the referee ran back to the halfway line, the Brighton players surrounded him in protest. Incredibly, the referee went back to consult with the same linesman and disallowed the goal, apparently for a foul by Rob Dewhurst. Unsurprisingly it infuriated Dolan and Martin Fish made an official complaint to the Football Association about the matter. He said, 'We cannot have situations where decisions are changed on the basis of protests.' The goalless draw we came away from the south coast with was unsatisfactory, in more ways than one, and virtually killed off any remaining hopes of getting into the play-offs.

City came back by beating Bradford City in a bad-tempered game at Boothferry in which Carl Shutt was sent off for stamping on Simon Dakin. City then took over 1,000 fans to Huddersfield on Easter Monday to try and hold the Third Division leaders. They managed that, even going in front through Dewhurst before Town equalised, the Tigers coming away with a creditable 1-1 draw.

Over 1,000 City fans descended on Blackpool for the final game of that season and it was a season that ended in high spirits with most fans believing that a slightly bigger squad, whilst holding onto the likes of Fettis and Windass, would give us an excellent chance of the play-offs in the following season. As a sign of the size of squad that Dolan had to cope with, Alan Fettis was once again used as a striker, though this time he played the full game, again doing very little throughout the game only to score the winner in injury time!

The only downside to the game was that the City players were not allowed onto the pitch after the game to salute the fans after a hard season. The thousand City fans had all stayed behind, sure that the players would be coming out, but the Blackpool police, for some reason, would not allow the players and staff past the halfway line, over fifty yards away from where the City fans were. It was a ridiculous decision and, once again, angered Martin Fish who said he would write to the police in Blackpool to complain.

Two seasons in a row the team had narrowly avoided reaching the play-offs; both times, arguably the size of the squad was to blame for the ultimate failure to progress. However, Martin Fish insisted that he did as much as he could to try and give the management duo as much help as possible in achieving that aim. He said: *'Promotion would have brought increased attendances as a result and that in itself would have got the ball rolling because I was hoping to get the debt cleared and I was moving in that direction because the crowds were reasonable. It was when the gates dropped that the real problems came in but I was all for getting in the First Division, as it was then.*

'I wouldn't interfere with the management but Terry knew where he stood in terms of players. I did say that if he did want extra ones, as long as we didn't pay a fortune then yes, have a look. But Terry was the type who would say, "I'm not just spending money for the sake of it" and unless it was a player who could definitely contribute to the side then he wouldn't do it, and I don't think he could find the right kind of players that he wanted.'

Jeff Radcliffe remains a fan of the management duo of the time, and says that they worked hard throughout to try and bring success to the club even though the club's financial situation made their job that much harder: *'Terry and Jeff Lee, whatever the fans might think, worked their socks off for the club. They were out every night watching reserve games, non-league games, trying to get players for nothing because they couldn't sign anyone for money. He's done well in the lower leagues and what happened at the end of his time was scandalous. The two of them with Martin put so much time and effort in. The fans' group has a lot to answer for because Martin wasn't a millionaire and worked so hard for the club. Behind the scenes the club was a real unit; it was a family sticking together. Everyone gave it everything even though we didn't have success.'*

So the season ended in disappointment, but to many, the squad had overachieved, given the lack of money and lack of depth to the squad. Only Jimmy Graham and Craig Lawford had been added to the squad and these two inexperienced players replaced two older hands in David Norton and Graeme Atkinson, who never quite fulfilled his potential at City and moved to Preston North End.

In addition, two other experienced squad members, Brian Mitchell and Steve Moran, both announced their retirement during the season and their departures meant that the likes of Simon Dakin, Neil Mann, Richard Peacock and Adam Lowthorpe were being pushed into action quicker than anticipated and had extended runs in the first team, when at most other clubs they would have been content to wait in the reserves.

City benefited by using the loan market well with Gary Lund, Ray Wallace, Warren Joyce, Paul Cox and Ian Ormondroyd all coming to the club at one stage or another, but all left, again with the club keen to sign some of them permanently, especially Joyce and Wallace. In addition, City lost other experienced players, notably David Mail and Greg Abbot, to injuries for much of the season, leading to Linton Brown and Dean Windass being the oldest members of the team on some occasions.

The close season saw Chris Hargreaves released, a decision that few City fans argued with, though mystifyingly to those who saw him play for City, he has forged a good career for himself since he left the Tigers, albeit in the lower divisions. David Mail was also released, a decision that was inevitable due to his worsening injury situation.

So the squad went off on their hols before pre-season training, though Simon Dakin did a fair impression of City the following season by falling more than 50ft down a lift shaft in Tenerife whilst he was there with Neil Mann, Rob Dewhurst, Gary Hobson and Adam Lowthorpe. He could have been killed but thankfully escaped with cracked ribs and bruised lungs.

Season 1995-96

The play-offs were the minimum requirement for the 1995-96 season. With a couple of near misses in the previous two campaigns, it was the least that the supporters expected and with players such as Andy Mason and Michael Quigley having been signed from Premier League clubs, Bolton Wanderers and Manchester City respectively, promotion was definitely the aim before the season kicked off.

Season ticket sales had reached 1,500, 40% up on the previous season and executive boxes at the ground had sold out, meaning another £40,000 in revenue, so there was an air of expectation around Boothferry Park. However, the season began badly on the field with a 1-0 defeat at home to Swindon Town, though the team were unlucky, having hit the woodwork three times before half-time. More misfortune saw new signing Michael Quigley breaking his leg in a game at Rotherham. The second home game saw our first win of the season, 2-1 over Blackpool, and City were briefly in mid-table but a horrible September brought three draws and two defeats along with another defeat, at Coventry in the Coca-Cola Cup.

By October it was clear that the expected revival was not coming and with crowds down to the 3,000 mark, debts were increasing and there was increasing transfer speculation, especially regarding the future of Dean Windass.

Martin Fish revealed that he was talking to Norwich City about Windass and added that two other Premier League teams were also interested in signing him. He also said that a First Division club had made an enquiry about Alan Fettis, though gloom about the impending loss of Fettis was tempered by the news that 17-year-old Roy Carroll, who had been recommended to the club by Fettis himself, had signed a three-year contract.

A sign that all was not well in the dressing room came when City drew 0-0 with Oxford in a dreadful game at Boothferry Park. Andy Mason, playing one of his first games for the club, came on as a second-half substitute only to be substituted himself 20 minutes later and replaced by Alan Fettis upfront! It was a humiliating moment for the young striker and supporters were angry at the treatment he had received from Dolan and Lee. Terry Dolan defended himself later, saying: '*He has to realise this is not Roy of the Rovers, it's not the Pontins League with Bolton Wanderers, it is the Second Division where you have to work very hard and do things right.*'

Dressing room morale was perhaps further hit when after a 2-0 defeat by Carlisle at Brunton Park, Dolan said, '*Without being too impolite, we looked exactly what we are - a team of free transfers and youngsters.*'

He was right, but it wasn't what supporters, and especially players, wanted to hear. We wanted to know what the manager was going to do about a season that was rapidly turning into a nightmare and which continued with a 3-0 home defeat by York

City. As chants of 'what a load of rubbish' echoed around the ground, the fans became ever more aware that the revival, which Dolan promised would come, had better happen quickly or the Tigers would become stranded at the bottom of the table.

Off the field, the situation was little better. Christopher Needler made a statement just before Christmas following calls for his resignation from disgruntled fans, saying, *'I continue as a director because I believe, in that position, I am better able to ensure that the club continues to function'.* Hardly the rousing message that City fans wanted but in truth few expected that from the board.

He had been forced to put his head above the parapet as Martin Fish had represented the club at yet another High Court appearance to try and prevent the club being wound up. He remembers: *Nobody knows financially just what was involved. I had to pay the players wages out of my pocket when bank managers froze bank accounts and the players knew what was going on. I think some of the worst moments were the visits to the High Court when the judge very nearly gave up on us. We had to defer it to the afternoon and put another submission in. The problem was that the money was going to come from the sale of Dean Windass, but I wasn't allowed to say that because that would have detracted from the deal and we wouldn't have got anything like the money that we did.*

'The judge was insisting that we disclose and I refused. There were Angie Rowe and her mates stuck in the back, not helping and they couldn't understand it. I had to box clever that day and it was a really worrying moment because we were on the verge of going under.'

Though the move to Norwich failed to go through, it was inevitable that Dean Windass was not going to stay with this sinking ship. He was too good for City at the time and deserved the chance to go to a bigger and better club, though it was a surprise for most of us to see that club as Aberdeen and for a price as low as £600,000. However, the money went to the Inland Revenue, keeping the club in existence a little longer though none would be given to Dolan to strengthen the team.

With Windass gone, the performances on the field continued to deteriorate and by March we were still rooted to the bottom of the table. One game against Chesterfield sticks in the memory. I was unable to go to the whole game so came in for free midway through the second half. There were probably 2,500 to 3,000 in the ground, though some had already gone and the standard of football, from both sides, was pitiful. The likes of Sheffield Wednesday had tried to improve the atmosphere at Hillsborough by introducing a band and, while most fans hated it, it was something which other clubs tried to imitate.

With the club bottom of the league, playing the worst football at Boothferry Park in living memory in front of crowds also at an all-time low, perhaps this wasn't the best time to introduce a drum into the ground in an attempt to 'improve the atmosphere'. However, it was there, in the Best Stand, for that game against Chesterfield and when I thought about the games and players I had seen at Boothferry Park, for it to be reduced to this was perhaps the most depressing spectacle during my time as a City fan. Worse even than the horrors to come.

There was no hope of avoiding the ignominy of relegation back to the old Fourth Division, though with eleven games left, Dolan did introduce some humour into the proceedings by saying that, *'With nine or ten wins we can still stay in the division and that is how we are looking at it.'*

Neil Mann and Richard Peacock both signed new three-year contracts at Boothferry Park but there were a couple of notable departures as Dolan tried to shake up the side towards the end of the season. Linton Brown, who had promised so much in the previous two seasons, was sold to Jan Molby at Swansea for £60,000 plus a 25% sell-on clause. It was hard to disagree with the manager when he said of the striker, *'It could be that a change will do him good because he was going nowhere quickly with us.'* It was true but begged the question, why did his career stall in such a dramatic way and how many other players at the time were 'going nowhere quickly with us'?

A week later Gary Hobson, who had been such a solid reliable defender for City, was sold to Brighton, also for £60,000 and City signed two new acquisitions, Duane Darby and Scott Maxfield, both from Doncaster.

LOOK BACK IN AMBER

With the team down and questions needing to be asked, the club was coming under fire from supporters who were amazed to hear that Martin Fish had banned *Hull Daily Mail* reporter Colin Young from attending the annual meeting between chairman, manager and members of the Southern Supporters club prior to our game away at Brighton.

The first of what were to be several more bans, the chairman said that it was because of the article in which Dean Windass had said he had learnt more in two weeks at Aberdeen than in two years at City. The Southern Supporters' meeting, when it did go ahead, heard that the chairman was preparing new contracts for Terry Dolan and Jeff Lee and revealed that the board was split between building a new 5,500 all-seater East Stand at Boothferry Park or moving to a new 6,000 all-seater ground near to Priory Park. The following day, with Ian Wilkinson making his debut, City lost 4-0.

The Tigers were effectively relegated by Easter but the drop was finally confirmed on April 13 when we lost at home to Crewe, quite a difference in fortune from the last time we played them at home. Then we had beat them 7-1 with more than an eye on the play-offs, now we were the first team in the country to be relegated. Why such an extraordinary decline?

Terry Dolan's comments in the aftermath of the relegation did not pacify supporters who were becoming increasingly troubled by the prospect of another season under the current regime, both in the boardroom and on the bench.

Dolan said: '*I am sure the club is in a far better state than it was two or three years ago. The sacrifice for making sure the club survived is Division Three football but hopefully it will give us a better platform to build from. True supporters need something to grab hold of now and hopefully that will come over the next few weeks.*'

Few supporters found the club in a better state than at practically any time in the club's history. We had just suffered our second relegation in five years and were in the bottom division for only the second time in our history, we had no money for players, no players of any value left at the club and no youngsters coming up through the ranks. However, nobody could argue with the final sentence in his quote. After such a demoralising season in which many had questioned what the point of following City was, we desperately needed something to look forward to going into the new season.

Martin Fish did not criticise his manager at the time, though he at least hints at it some ten years later. He said:

'We had become rather ultra-defensive. We were trying to not let any goals in and if we got one at the other end that was great. That isn't attractive for supporters to watch. The Boothferry Park crowds always used to get at one player or another and I don't think that helped at all. But there were no problems within the club at that time, it is very hard to put your finger on why things started to go wrong. Nothing had changed, the management hadn't changed and most of the players hadn't, perhaps it was the rub of the green. Things got tighter later on and that was solely monetary and when you start to lose your better players, you are going to go down.'

With relegation now secured, events off the field became more important to supporters than achieving any sort of respectability in the last few games. We desperately needed to know that there were people who wanted to buy the club off Needler. Part of this problem was secured later in April when Needler and Chetham announced that they would be leaving the board and that Needler was to transfer all his shares to Martin Fish. He added: *'He will then be the sole shareholder of the non-voting shares that control the company in certain circumstances, in particular the sale of the ground or moving soccer away from Boothferry Park.'*

However, the club would still be in the hands of those answerable to Needler and what the fans desperately wanted was someone hitherto unconnected with the club, untainted by the past, who had a vision for the future.

The season had been a disaster; we were bottom going into the last game with just 31 points, nine behind second bottom Brighton and eighteen points away from safety. We had won just five games all season and scored just 34 goals, by far the lowest in the division. We had conceded 75 goals; only Swansea, who were relegated with us, had let in more. So this was the situation going into our final game of the season, at home to a Bradford City side who were aiming for the play-offs. It was a bitter pill to swallow for City fans as the two clubs were comparable in many ways.

We had gone up into the old Second Division together in the mid-Eighties, the year of the terrible fire at Valley Parade and, for a brief and glorious time, we were first and second in that division. It was humiliating enough playing host to Bradford whilst already relegated and them so obviously on the way up with an ambitious chairman; it was made worse, much much worse by giving their supporters the South Stand.

The decision had been made that, for the first time in the club's history, City fans would not be able to watch a home game from the South Stand. The old Bunkers Hill would be full of Bradford fans with City supporters reduced to watching from the supermarket end with a few in the East Stand.

The club had been building up to this decision for some little time, giving the East Stand over to Bolton and Sheffield Wednesday when they brought big support with them, but this was far worse. After the season we had had, it was seen as the ultimate kick in the teeth for the long-suffering fans and the temperature reached boiling point on that horrible day in May 1996.

The anger at the time was largely with Martin Fish, supporters hardly needing another stick to beat him with. However, he maintains that the affair was not of his making. '*The Bradford game was a horrible catastrophic situation which was a gun to my head by the police. My hands were totally tied. Bryan Calam was the match commander and he rang me on the Tuesday and said he thought the only way we could stage the match was by switching the ends. I said, "You are joking, I will be annihilated if I do that." He went to see his boss, came back down to the club and said that if we didn't move the home fans they would not police it in the true sense of the word and anything that happened would be our personal responsibility.*

'*He said it would be much better for gate receipts, but I said I wasn't thinking about gate receipts but about our supporters. Subsequently I think Bryan Calam went in the* Hull Daily Mail *to say that it wasn't my fault, which was the truth. I would never have done that off my own bat, gate receipts or not.*

THE DOLAN YEARS

'I knew Geoffrey Richmond fairly well at Bradford and he was pressing for the switch too. He said that they would fill the stand for us but I told him that I had to think about our own supporters. He replied that they didn't think much about me. It was terrible. Bryan Calam was playing a crafty game though because as soon as we sold the club to David Lloyd he was straight in, trying to help him and got a fairly cushy number with him.'

John Cooper backs the chairman in his version of events: 'The Bradford game was another piece of unwelcome history. There was never any intelligence to suggest that Bradford were going to bring a large number of fans. Bryan Calam, the match commander, phoned up the club on the Wednesday morning after Bradford had played Swindon. He said that we had a problem and said that Bradford would bring more fans than the North Stand would hold. So I suggested that we give them the North Stand, open up the North East corner and if we had to we would have to work round to giving them the East Stand. Everyone seemed happy with that but on the Thursday Geoffrey Richmond was banging the drum, urging their supporters to travel to Hull as they needed the points to get into the play-offs.

'Martin had his own business to run so he used to come into the club only on some days. On the Thursday he was here and Bryan Calam phoned to ask for an urgent meeting between Bryan, Martin and myself. He said that Bradford were going to bring 8,000 and what were we going to do about it? My first reaction was to ask Martin to phone the Football League to see if we could make the game all-ticket and play the game on the Sunday, but we couldn't do that as every game had to kick off at the same time, being the last game of the season. Had the intelligence been that way, the game would definitely have been all-ticket, but we couldn't implement an all-ticket game with that length of time.

'So Bryan Calam said to Martin that to stop the problems he wanted him to hand over the home end, the South Stand, to Bradford. Martin said, '"No way, I'll be lynched," but Bryan said in roundabout terms that if he didn't they wouldn't police the game. Martin turned the colour of the wall, which was magnolia, and whichever way we went we couldn't win because we had to have the police there.

LOOK BACK IN AMBER

'I've still got a tape of the match here in my office and I keep it as a reminder to people who want to see the dark days. All people could see was Martin thinking about getting as many people in the ground as he could, getting a fat back pocket. Nobody could tell the City fans anything, they believed what they wanted to believe.'

Whatever the rights and wrongs, the day, described at the time by Martin Fish as 'my worst nightmare" was seen as a final humiliation by City fans who had been forced to endure one of the worst seasons in the club's history and furious City fans inundated the Boothferry Park switchboard as well as the offices of the *Hull Daily Mail* sports desk.

Someone said to me on the day of the game, 'This game won't finish'. It was highly-charged and there was great anger on the North terrace but even the pitch invasions summed up the state of the club at the time. One before kick-off and then another couple whilst the match was taking place, they were half-hearted and even though the police presence at the north end of the ground wasn't too restrictive, it appeared that many supporters shrugged their shoulders, accepted the situation as best they could and watched what entertainment there was in the course of the game.

It was actually a quite good game with a young City team giving Bradford quite a scare, though you always felt that however many City scored, Bradford were well capable of going down the other end and getting a goal themselves. Duane Darby and Gavin Gordon scored for the Tigers and worked well together, looking capable of making an impression the following season, a tiny crumb of comfort for those of us who would be back to Boothferry Park when City would start the campaign to try and win promotion back to the Second Division.

Towards the end of the relegation season, chairman Martin Fish promised a big announcement which, he assured fans, they would be happy with. The announcement involved demolishing the East Stand terracing and building a brand new 5,000 all-seater stand on that side of Boothferry Park with plans for executive boxes to increase revenue. Fish said that he would apply to the Football Licensing Authorities for loans to cover most of the funding for the stand but appealed to local businesses for help.

THE DOLAN YEARS

If that had been the end of the announcement, few would have argued. It was uninspiring and many doubted whether the stand would be built, but Fish continued and, at the end of a season which had seen crowds plummet to new lows amid a constant backdrop of criticism of manager Terry Dolan and assistant Jeff Lee, Fish said that the pair were to be given new three-year contracts, even though their existing contracts still had a year to run. There had been talk of the pair being given new contracts but as the season progressed and relegation confirmed, very few expected them to be granted. It was a decision which mystified supporters and led directly to a year-long often vitriolic campaign to oust both the management duo and the chairman himself.

Despite the ramifications of his decision, Fish still does not feel he made a misjudgement:

'I don't regret giving them extended contracts. OK, I might have been wrong, it's for others to judge me, but I myself don't feel I did anything wrong. I simply renewed their contracts because they could have gone at the end of that season and then we would have started with someone else, which would have involved compensation to the other club depending on who we got, and the club was not in a position to afford that kind of thing.

'To me it was the cheapest option to just renew their contracts because I didn't want to go on spending money on a new management team. I had the Revenue on my back and they were not easy people to deal with. Paying off contracts would just have costed too much.

'I also felt that yes, we had gone down but the fellows themselves didn't do a lot wrong. They had generated a fair amount of money in transfer fees with Windass, Fettis and so on and the kind of players he found such as Roy Carroll, who Terry and Jeff found in Ireland with Fettis.

'However, the crowd were not prepared to wait, they had all these years of promises and so on but I wasn't prepared to give promises; I didn't want to do that to the crowd, it wasn't fair to the supporters. Why give them promises that you can't keep? I might have got criticised heavily for it but what I said to people, I felt was the truth.

'I still had faith in Terry Dolan to turn things round. He went off to Huddersfield, then York and I could see there what he was doing. He got York into eighth position and then got the sack so he's not exactly had the best of luck in the way things have happened, and again it was a financial situation in that they couldn't afford his salary at York. I knew what he could do, I knew what he had generated, some £2m in transfer fees out of nothing. So it might not have been pretty playing on the pitch but it was doing a job behind the scenes and it was just that we needed more time.'

However, Martin Fish does concede that other managers were in his thoughts if he ever was in a position to sack Dolan and Lee. He comments: *'Gregor Rioch, who came to the club at this time, was a character and I met his father a few times. I think if I had had to replace Terry Dolan it might have been Bruce Rioch that I would have gone for. Not that the situation ever arose but he was the type of manager I would have been looking for. He was a disciplinarian and that was important.'*

Season 1996-97

The summer of 1996 saw the Tigers once again in the basement division but this time, arguably, with less hope than the previous time. In 1982 there were a crop of youngsters ready to take their place in the first team and move the team back up the divisions. This time there were no signs of any promising youngsters coming through with many feeling that youth development had been neglected during Dolan's time in charge.

With such anger at the way the club was being run on and off the field, Tigers 2000 was born with the campaign group asking questions of the accounts, the sale of the railway plaque, the banning of David Bond, the former *Mail* sports writer from the ground and the terrible and dramatic decline of the club during the past year. The group clamoured for Christopher Needler to come out from behind Martin Fish and confront the issues surrounding the club and the ground.

THE DOLAN YEARS

Relations between club and supporters were reaching breaking point and some fans went to extremes. Tigers 2000 tried to spread their message on an open-top bus tour of the city with stops at Boothferry Park and at the homes of Terry Dolan and Martin Fish. It's a subject that still pains Fish to this day.

'The tour bus was probably one of the worst things, that was the one thing when my wife said, really you've got to be out of this. The situation was they were going to have this tour on an open-topped bus going through the streets of the city, and they would travel up to North Ferriby which is where I and Terry Dolan live. I alerted the police and told them I wanted cover from the police because I didn't know what I would be faced with. They reassured me by saying that they had it covered with plain-clothed officers and unmarked vehicles.

'My wife and daughter were just going out to town and had just got to the garage to get to the car when this bus arrived outside the house. The two of them were stuck in the car and I told them not to get out. I got straight onto the police asking what had gone on and they said there had been a change of shift and, between the shifts and change of vehicles, this bus had got through. I alerted Terry to tell him to get out of the way, which he did.

'Angie Rowe had this big loudspeaker saying why I had to resign and all the rest. My neighbours couldn't believe it; I even got cards from the neighbours to say this was so unfair. It shouldn't affect your home life and when it does things are seriously wrong, but that was the level they were getting to.'

That wasn't an end to the abuse handed out to the chairman. In July 1996 a group of fans claimed responsibility after a jar of maggots wrapped in a 'Fish out' poster was stuffed through the club's letterbox. It was possibly the same group of fans who posted a cod's head to the offices of Darlington, City's first opponents at the start of the 1996-97 season with the message 'Get rid of Fish'. Fish remembers:

'When I heard that they were going to send a cod's head through the post to every away chairman that the club was going to visit, I wrote a letter to all the clubs to alert them. Jimmy Hill, who was chairman of Fulham at the time, wrote back and thanked me for alerting them and said that whilst it didn't bother them, it was a bit mean that they wouldn't be sending the rest of the fish!'

LOOK BACK IN AMBER

John Cooper was witness to that time and felt for the chairman: '*Martin had the club at heart and I clearly remember the abuse that he got from the fans. The cods' heads were sent up to Darlington, Hartlepool and other clubs. I used to open all the mail and never let Martin open any because some of the things coming through the post were nothing short of scandalous. The real low points were getting some maggots through the club's letterbox, some excrement also coming through the letterbox, and the one thing that really hurt was the open-topped bus to his house in Ferriby.*

'*I understood the frustrations of fans when things were not going right but there was a line of demarcation that we all must operate to. One was legal, the other was illegal and I thought that was illegal. There was also the attack on the pitch which hurt me more than anything. Somebody came in overnight and daubed "Fish out" in huge white letters. I lost my cool because at the time there were groups of supporters who were whipping things up around the city and I thought that they were responsible for the damage, maybe not directly, but indirectly.*

'*I voiced my opinion about the outrage only to find a piece in the* Hull Daily Mail *and in the fanzine which implied it was done professionally. I took legal action and I fought it my own way because I felt it was my reputation on the line. I felt somebody was indirectly accusing me of implementing that and it was so far off the mark. I took it as far as I could because I was paying for it myself. The club did offer to pay but I refused because it was my fight and my reputation.*'

The 1996-97 season itself began with a great Duane Darby hat-trick in a 3-2 home win against Darlington in front of just over 4,000. However, after eight more games the side had scored just five more goals and although fifth in the table, there was renewed unrest on the terraces as Scunthorpe United came to town.

The team for the Scunthorpe game was Wilson, Trevitt, Rioch, Allison, Wright, Brien, Joyce, Quigley, Darby, Mann and Gordon, and the wheels came off City's season that afternoon as the Tigers put in a terrible performance, the Iron deservedly winning 2-0. The whole of the second half was played with constant noise from the home fans calling for Fish and Dolan to go. The game was even held up for a couple of minutes as four City fans went on to the pitch in protest whilst many others left early to congregate at the back of the Best Stand. Hundreds stayed for about an hour to demonstrate at the state of the club.

The *Mail* was full of the protests on the following Monday with Martin Fish, referring to the fact that the defeat was the first for City in 11 matches, saying, 'I would have thought our supporters would have been cock-a-hoop about that.'

Soon after the Scunthorpe game the club 'celebrated' 50 years at Boothferry Park. Given the club's standing it was never going to be a tumultuous celebration and any chances of it being so were reduced further with the news that Ken Wagstaff and Chris Chilton, probably the club's greatest living legends, were banned from attending by Martin Fish.

He said that he had decided not to invite the pair because Wagstaff had been appointed president of Tigers 2000 and he had 'gone out on a limb and criticised Fish'. He added that Chilton had done the same, probably at Wagstaff's request, so the big day saw just nine ex-players presented to the crowd, a jazz band and a small balloon release before kick-off. Not surprisingly it failed to inspire the Tigers who played out a goalless draw with Barnet.

The season continued in similar vein with poor performances on the field interspersed with gloom off it. Martin Fish admitted that the club were £500,000 in debt and losing £5,000 a week and was forced to confirm stories first uncovered by Tigers 2000 that the Hull City brass nameplate which had been over the players' tunnel for so many years had been sold two years previously and replaced by a plastic version.

Tom Wilson remembers the sale: '*One of the things we did do was get rid of the Hull City sign above the tunnel. I didn't think it would be missed because before it was taken down I had it replaced with a new one which just looked as if it had been polished up. There were only two people who knew about that sign, myself and Martin Fish, and I never told a soul about it but it eventually got out so it could have only been one person.*

LOOK BACK IN AMBER

'I was offered £1,500 for it initially because I got in touch with the railway museum in York and they put me in touch with a couple of people who are collectors of that type of memorabilia. I think we got up to about four or £5,000 but I left it because I thought we could still get a better price for it. There were no computers in those days to log onto eBay to see what we could get!

'Eventually someone came back in for it and I got about £12,000 for it. I just handed it over to the person I was supposed to hand it to and that was the end of the matter as far as I was concerned. The plastic one that replaced it didn't cost us a penny as it was part of the deal. Martin had nothing to do with it, I did the deal but he knew what was going on as I never did anything without running it past him first.'

Demonstrations against the management and board continued and a few weeks later about 400 supporters staged a walk-out after about 70 minutes of a home game against Fulham which saw City lose 3-0. The demonstrators continued their protests in Boothferry Road for about an hour after the game.

A brief on-field respite included City progressing in the FA Cup, though they came within minutes of going out to Whitby Town, a club goodness knows how many leagues below the Tigers. The teams drew 0-0 in the original tie, held at Scarborough's ground. However, at Boothferry Park, Whitby went into a 4-3 lead, which they held until the dying seconds of the game before City equalised to take the tie into extra time and greater fitness told as the Tigers ran out 8-4 winners with Duane Darby scoring four.

As the season progressed more news of possible takeovers of the club began to leak out. Boxing promoter Frank Maloney was among those who expressed an interest in taking control of the club though he stopped short of an intention to buy City outright. His plans included appointing ex-Chelsea player Alan Hudson as manager and Maloney himself would act as an intermediary between the manager and the board. Few thought his interest would come to anything but fans were excited by the possible reappearance of Don Robinson who had also expressed an interest.

He gave details of a takeover package which included £1m for team and club improvements, an offer to take over a maximum

£500,000 debt at the bank, a pledge to build a new East Stand and a restructuring of the club's shares. He appeared to have Martin Fish on his side and Richard Chetham also welcomed the move, stressing that he would support it at the forthcoming board meeting.

However, the man who held all the cards, Christopher Needler, refused to accept the deal, seemingly because he wanted to keep control of the ground. He said:

'It is against my family wishes that the ground is bought by property developers and I want that protected for the future. Don has tried to buy them in the past.'

The news led to the resignation of Richard Chetham from the board, leaving just Fish and Needler as directors.

Fish remembers: *'There was a problem between Christopher Needler and Don Robinson and he wasn't going to let Don back in. I don't know what happened when the club went into receivership but Don was the saviour and brought the club out of it, what that deal was between the two of them, I don't know but there was something there that was saying to Christopher, no not again. I don't even know if it was a financial issue or a personal thing between the two of them, but the two men didn't exactly hit it off at all.*

'Christopher stayed on the board throughout Don's time because that was one of the conditions of the deal, but it created problems. I kept on putting Don's interests forward but the Needler family held the voting power. He said that those shares should be cancelled but I said to him that they weren't and we had to look at realistic things. I said that whilst the Needler family had the power, I could not do anything more for him.'

Don Robinson himself claimed that there was much paper talk regarding his possible reappearance. He said: *'Martin Fish is a really nice guy and when I was with him you couldn't wish for a better colleague, but I think when he was in charge of the whole thing, it was too much and I think a few people took him for a ride. The press had something to do with my possible return to the club. I had wanted to help out a little and suddenly it was all about me coming back to the club, which I couldn't really have done because of other work commitments.'*

However, Needler was still looking to sever his family's long connection with Hull City, entrusting Martin Fish to secure any deal. Fish remembers:

'I might not have received praise for it but we have still got a club for other people to take on. Adam Pearson could not have done anything without a registered club, which is all that I was there for really, just to hold it together so we could get a deal done. The Needlers had said by this time that they wanted to sell. I was keen to get away myself because of the personal abuse I was getting, but I was itching to carry on in a way to show them that I could get through it.

''The turning point for me was the East Stand situation. I felt I had done so much work to get it moving and for very little cost and getting it built would have lifted the supporters. They would have had a supporters' club and things may have turned. But at the time I did that Christopher Needler came and said that he had had enough so asked me to try and sell the club and I was left to try and find a buyer.

The off the field distractions did not hide the fact that the season itself was turning into another failure with early promise of a play-off place at the very least fading from the memory, with City poised to finish in their worst league position ever. The only thing that was keeping the supporters going was the hope and belief that Fish and Dolan would soon be leaving Boothferry Park for good.

By May 1997, as the season neared its end, Christopher Needler was forced to deny claims that he had already agreed a deal to sell the club after Tim Wilby, the chairman of the Hull Sharks, said that this was the reason for him dropping his own interest in buying the club.

He insisted that Needler had signed a deal with a mystery consortium and that as a result, Wilby had withdrawn his own offer from the negotiating table. Wilby said that he had hoped to become chairman of the club before overseeing the building of a new super-stadium to house both the Sharks and Hull City.

As the final game of a disappointing season approached and the papers were full of takeover talk, including the crucial question of whether or not Christopher Needler had it in his mind to sell the ground, Tigers 2000 demanded answers from him on whether the

THE DOLAN YEARS

Scarborough game, the last game of the season, would be the last Hull City game to be played at Boothferry Park.

City fans certainly wanted the game to be Dolan's last, at least as City manager, and cries of 'Dolan out' came from all quarters of the ground for almost the full 90 minutes. It was only a heavy police presence which stopped some fans from getting onto the pitch and more than a hundred fans congregated outside the Best Stand at the end of the game to chant and demonstrate against the chairman and manager.

On the field in 1996-97 Duane Darby was the hero, scoring over 20 goals for the club whilst Gavin Gordon showed some promise for a 17-year-old, as he did at the end of the 1995-96 season. The two of them appeared to have the makings of a decent strike partnership. Richard Peacock was also tried up front and though he didn't look the part as a striker, seemed to have enough flair to suggest that he could have a part to play in any City revival, especially in a wide position.

Ian Wright was probably the most consistent defender whilst Gregor Rioch also played well for the club but Rob Dewhurst, who had appeared to be a real find when he first came to the side from Blackburn, had seen his form deteriorate badly. The priority for whoever was in charge of the team the following season would be experienced forwards who could hold the ball up along with a creative midfielder. With these additions, it was felt that City could have the makings of a successful side in 1997-98 in what was a very poor Third Division.

Terry Dolan went public in saying, as the season drew to an end, that he hoped whoever the new owners were, they would give him a chance to prove himself as manager. He said he hoped to be given the chance to buy a new team to get the club out of the Third Division and added that he had never been given the chance to show what he could do with money at his disposal. He said: '*I want the opportunity to show what I can do and I would put myself up against anybody else. For six years we have kept the club going by having to sell players and bringing them in for very little value.*'

He said that if he had been allowed to spend some money in 1995 on loan players Ormondroyd, Lund, Ray Wallace and Warren Joyce, he could have built a successful side and that to add those players to the likes of Fettis, Windass and Brown, who were already at the club, City could have had a side capable of achieving promotion.

He may well have had a point about team-strengthening when the Windass/Brown partnership was at its height, but having endured the past couple of season there were few fans willing to give him another chance and there was no common ground whatsoever between the supporters and Dolan/Fish.

Danny Fullbrook, *Mail* correspondent said: '*Obviously the two groups are poles apart and have completely different opinions about what is going on. The supporters' campaign has become very personal and hateful, especially towards Dolan, but then again at no stage during the season have the club ever tried to communicate with the fans and show any willingness to listen to their grievances. There is not now a mediator in the land who could bring these two sides together.*

'*The simple truth is that 17th position in the Third Division is the worst final league position in the club's history. This fact alone means it is time for change, which could be on the horizon. Dolan's job has not been just about money but motivation. He has simply not produced the goods and in a high profile position where success is paramount, managers should expect to be shown the door.*'

He also criticised Needler, who he accused of passing the buck. He said that Needler had the funds to make a difference at the club but did not have the inclination to give the city the club it deserved. '*He admits to being more interested in gardening than football but forgets that the best piece of grass in the city was the pitch at Boothferry Park and he could have provided the team to go with it. City's fifty-year-old stadium is one of the newest in the country, built by his father Harold for the Tigers supporters but his son has allowed it to become a dilapidated eyesore with many areas unsafe to use.*'

However, salvation was at hand and Christopher Needler's long and ultimately unsuccessful time with Hull City was coming to an end. So was Martin Fish's time as chairman. He explains: '*David Lloyd's interest first came through on a phone call from a group of people. There had been an interest in Hull Kingston Rovers from Tim Wilby who had Hull FC and was looking at Rovers. The person who made that approach then contacted me completely out of the blue and asked if there would there be any chance of talking about the possibility of taking the club over. The next approach was from Tim Wilby who said that he would like to talk to me. He said that the interest was from David Lloyd as well as himself but that he would be running it for Lloyd.*

'Fortunately David Lloyd had the money but it was a traumatic time. Wilby was not an easy character to deal with at all and there was a lot of unpleasant background stuff, threats of getting beaten up and all sorts. It was very unsavoury. We met at a Northampton hotel and someone said to me that if I didn't get the deal pushed through I may end up in a heap one day. Incredible stuff really.'

PART SIX

Lock-outs

Season 1997-98

The summer of 1997 finally saw an end to the Needler family's involvement in Hull City. In June 1997, after months of speculation on the future of the club, it was announced that David Lloyd was to complete a £2.5m takeover of Hull City when, along with Tim Wilby, he bought Christopher Needler's 64% shareholding in the club.

However, to add to the shock for those at Boothferry Park, an old face was also involved in the deal. John Cooper remembers the time: *'The first point of contact I had with the Lloyd regime was actually Bryan Calam again. In February of that year he had approached me about getting a job at Boothferry Park. I'd worked with him for quite a few years and he was a very good match commander, one of the best I'd worked with. He said that we worked well together and that he was thinking of leaving the police force because of ill health and wondered about becoming safety officer at the club. I couldn't dispute his credentials and I said I would have a word with Martin.*

''I said to Martin that he had offered himself but he knew I wasn't comfortable about something. I couldn't put my finger on what it was but suggested to Martin that he meet Calam and if he felt he was the right man for the job to appoint him and forget my feelings. After meeting he said to me that he knew what I meant. So that process never carried on although Calam was still involved with the club through his work with the police. In the meantime, Bryan played a lot of golf and had been talking with Tim Wilby on the courses around Hull.

'Wilby was caretaker of a block of flats in Chelsea but a lot of people up here were told that he was into property, so you can take that which way you want. The next thing I knew was a meeting with Bryan Calam who revealed this time that he was involved with David Lloyd. He said that he had been offered a job with David Lloyd and wanted us to work together.'

However, supporters had not quite seen the back of Messrs Fish and Dolan. Due to the takeover being delayed slightly, Terry

Dolan, still being the team manager at this point, came back to the club to oversee the first few days of pre-season training, though it was obvious to all, including himself, that he would not be with the club when the new season was due to start.

Finally, in July, just as the players were due to step up their pre-season training, the deal was secured and Martin Fish walked out of the Boothferry Park chairman's office for the last time. It was a strange feeling for him: '*By the time I came out of it I thought that at least I'd kept the club alive and I've done my bit for society. I also thought at the time that it was a good deal for the club. One of the conditions I put on any deal was that he paid the creditors, the bank, the Inland Revenue, Customs & Excise, debenture holders and general creditors. Normally in those kind of deals, you leave it to the purchaser to buy them off, but I wasn't trusting them too much, so I said that I wanted the money paid into our solicitor's so that we paid off the creditors, and we could see that it had been done.*

'*Eventually they did it so I knew that everybody had been paid. Lloyd talked well about what he was going to do with the club. He had sold his David Lloyd tennis centres to Whitbread and got a lot of money for them. Some of this money was allocated to this deal and he was also going to put in another million or two. I knew he had it and it demonstrated that he had it because he was willing to do this transaction of paying us so that we could pay others off. He talked about how he was going to develop the ground, put money in and so on and I had no reason to not think that he could not do it.*

So I left and leaving the club once the deal was complete was very sad for me. It had been such a rollercoaster ride, especially towards the end, but I remember looking out over Boothferry Park, over the pitch just before leaving for the last time, and I had tears in my eyes. It was sad but there was also some relief because the pressure on me was intense.'

Though the pressure of being in the hot seat at Boothferry Park had come to an end, he could never escape from the experience he had endured over the past ten years and it was apparent that many City fans could not forgive or forget Fish's time as chairman. He said: '*I couldn't support the club afterwards and I've only been* back twice, even though I've supported them since 1950. I didn't go back under Lloyd because he said it was for the best and he wanted a completely fresh situation. There was only Mrs Needler who I think was allowed to go into the directors' room, so I kept away. I thought that was fair enough, they had to have time to do their own thing. Then Tom Belton came in, who I knew because he was chairman at Scunthorpe at the same time as I had been chairman at City.

'So he invited me to a game and I was in the directors' box and they were hanging over the box, saying what the hell are you here for? This was about two years after I'd left the club. I thought, "They are not going to forget and it's for the best if I stay away." I was still being shouted at when I left the ground underneath the West Stand.

'I still now can't go into town shopping with my wife. I once went into Princes Quay with her and I had to separate her and put her in a shop and it's now eight years since I left the club. Also, it was only last year that I walked out to my car at work and a car drove up and these lads started shouting at me, saying, "This is what you've bought with the club's money is it?" You thieving individual and so on. I was showing a client out and he stayed in his car until the trouble was over. He couldn't believe that I was still getting abuse after all this time.'

Rob Smith, who worked for the club throughout all the time of Fish's chairmanship, pleads the case for the defence: 'Martin was obviously a supporter and thought a lot about the club. I think his hands were tied very much because of outside influences but he certainly gave the club so much time, despite having a business of his own in the city. Outside of his own office hours I reckon he was putting in another 8 to 10 hours a day running the football club. It must have destroyed him when he had to let go because he put so much personal time and effort in. I think that knowing that he was putting so much effort in made a few of us a bit stronger.'

However, the Fish chairmanship was at an end and, with his feet now under the chairman's desk at Boothferry Park as well as the Boulevard, Tim Wilby set about putting his plans into motion. Though David Lloyd was the owner, he had not been seen in Hull.

LOOK BACK IN AMBER

His voice in the city was Wilby and it was the former rugby league player, already chairman at the Hull Sharks, who immediately reiterated his intention, which was to build a new 20,000 all-seater stadium in the city which would be home to both City and the Hull Sharks Rugby League club, adding that in the short term, this would see City moving out of Boothferry Park to ground share at the Boulevard.

In hindsight the timing of this announcement was superb as the fans were so relieved to see the back of Fish and Dolan that Wilby would still have been cheered to the rafters whatever he had said.

There was also a new manager to appoint. To the surprise of nobody at all, Terry Dolan and Jeff Lee were relieved of their services and speculation was rife on who would be the new City manager with the new season only a month or so away. The only names that the new regime wanted were big ones, so anyone in the bottom two divisions, whatever their credentials, were immediately ruled out.

Peter Beardsley and Chris Waddle were the front-runners, certainly with the media, but the new face was to be an old team-mate of theirs, ex-Rangers and England forward Mark Hateley. He had left Queens Park Rangers in ignominy a few months earlier but he was still a sufficiently big name to excite the City faithful and, perhaps most important of all, his name was not Terry Dolan.

Hateley had an international career including 32 England caps, seven championship medals, six of which came at Rangers and the other at Monaco, where he was managed by Arsene Wenger and his team-mates included Glenn Hoddle. He had impeccable contacts and was at a stage where he was ready to cut down on playing and concentrate on management. With him came Billy Kirkwood, a well-respected coach from Scotland.

The personnel changes were not just on the field. We had Ian McMahon as chief executive and Nigel Kaye as marketing manager and all who came to the club spoke of how they were aiming to take the club higher than it had ever been before. It all came as quite a culture shock to the staff at the club. They had become used to the chairmanship of Martin Fish who had never been one for hyperbole, but now it was pouring out of the club every day.

LOCK-OUTS

Rob Smith experienced it first-hand: '*The first vision I had of Tim Wilby was when he came into the office. It was a transitional period and we knew that we had new owners coming in, but hadn't yet met them. Suddenly this strapping lad walks in with holiday shorts and sandals and sits with his feet up on the desk saying, right this is what I want you to do, this is what I'm going to do, hiring and firing, literally six yards in front of me.*

'*That was an awakening because I'd never dealt with people like that before. I worked with Martin Fish and others who were far gentler sort of people, not quite as ruthless on the outside. This new lot came in with all guns blazing, though they had done their homework and had started the process some time earlier with the takeover at Hull FC. It was like that for the first few months until some of those people were shipped out to other parts of the world quite quickly and it steadied a little bit.*

'*When a lot of people moved on at the start of that time, I suddenly had to reassume some of those roles just to get the club through the early days. There was a period before David Lloyd came to Hull when it was just Tim Wilby and his people. They didn't have any football experience; didn't know how to sign players on, didn't know about contracts. I had an idea just through making it my business to get to know these sorts of jobs, so there was a period of about six months whilst they got their staffing sorted out when I assumed the role of marketing manager.*

'*There was a high turnover of staff at that time and because they had brought in a number of people from other parts of the country, it was like a hurricane sweeping through the stadium really. I got moved down to the Boulevard where I was working from a converted bar, trying to work for Hull City but with a joint responsibility for the rugby, which is what David Lloyd wanted.*'

John Cooper, who had been associated with the club for several years and had spent so much time improving the pitch at Boothferry Park, was particularly concerned when Tim Wilby introduced himself at a tumultuous City Hall and announced that City would soon be moving into a new all-seater stadium, though in the meantime they would move away from Boothferry Park and play games at the Boulevard.

LOOK BACK IN AMBER

He says: '*I was edgy, having never met Lloyd at this time and I wanted to know in what direction they were taking the club. Statements had been released saying we are going to do this, do that, build this stadium, and I had also stood at the back of the famous meeting when Tim Wilby addressed Hull City supporters in the City Hall, saying that the club would move to the Boulevard for a short time and that he'd spoken to me about it. I'd never met the man. So there was a guy stood up in front of 5,000 people and I'm there with my name having been mentioned and I can't say anything.*'

Whatever the misgivings of those existing members of staff who were experiencing life under a new regime, for most City fans it was a glorious pre-season. Evidence that the club was now a more professionally run outfit was seen in many ways. Hell, the club even advertised the pre-season games in the *Daily Mail*! On the field too, the pre-season games were encouraging. The club were playing slick passing football, such a relief after the years of hoof and run we had been used to. The excitement grew and on a boiling hot day over 2,000 City fans arrived at Field Mill for the first game of the new season.

With representatives in the directors' box, a team of coaching staff looking the business in crisp white outfits, it was a relief to see the club at least looking the part after years of neglect and negativity. However, it took about five minutes of the game to realise that not everything had changed. We were certainly not going to have a promotion season to look forward to as most of us had hoped. We had prettier football admittedly, lots of running in neat patterns, but still defeats. We lost the Mansfield game 2-0 and deserved to. It could well be a long season ahead.

Despite the bad start to the season, plans were ongoing for the club to leave Boothferry Park for good in the November of 1997. The site would be sold and both the football club and the rugby club would play at the Boulevard until a new stadium was built. For John Cooper, there was the concern that the Boothferry Park pitch had been worked on for so many years to bring it up to the standard that he himself required, but he had real doubts as to whether he could perform the same magic on the pitch at the

LOCK-OUTS

Boulevard, especially with both the rugby and football teams due to play on it.

He says: '*I couldn't stop the football club moving to the Boulevard and if it had have been for the right reasons people would have accepted it, but I knew it wasn't for the right reasons. There was something about selling Boothferry Park that mattered. For some reason they had to sell it quickly.*

'*It was the speed at which things were being done that perhaps indicated that things weren't quite right. At a meeting I was told that we needed to be playing professional football at the Boulevard by November 5. Because I had built up quite a good relationship with the Football League by this time, I rang someone down there and asked him to fax me the minimum criteria on standards of professional football pitches. I put a plan together to drain the Boulevard pitch and obviously worked very closely with the rugby club. However, the rugby club knew that whatever happened their pitch would be improved as it was in a bad state at that time, but to get it to the required standard for football to be played there on November 5 would have needed drastic action.*

'*Whilst we were doing work on the Boulevard pitch, Hull FC were due to play a couple of matches at Boothferry Park. I remember Alan Mason of Hull FC telling me that they were losing thousands by not playing the match at the Boulevard because people just wouldn't watch rugby at Boothferry Park. So Hull went back to the Boulevard and we bought ourselves some time. They were very important days because I heard that David Lloyd was coming up and it was the same week that City were playing at home to Notts County in the first home game of the season.*'

It was David Lloyd's first public appearance at Boothferry Park and, despite the team losing at Mansfield the previous week, there was great optimism amongst the supporters. Money had been promised for new players; there were stories linking City with the likes of Andy Goram and Ally McCoist, old team-mates of Hateley's from his Rangers days, so it was hoped that the previous week's tame defeat could be put down to first night nerves.

John Cooper saw Lloyd's appearance in Hull as the last chance to persuade him that a move to the Boulevard would be a mistake.

LOOK BACK IN AMBER

So he set about his plans. He said: '*My words to the ground staff were, "Let's make it like the centre court," so the grass was cut at a certain height and it was presented in a certain way. The lines were immaculate as always but extra marked to make sure. I knew that if he came out and looked at the pitch he would want to walk on it. If he was a sportsman as everyone knew him as, he would want to walk on it.*

'*So I watched him from the players' tunnel. He came out onto the West Stand from the restaurant and then came down and as soon as he stepped out onto the pitch I went over and introduced myself. My words to him were, "Why do you want to move from here? I can resurrect this place if you want me to." He suddenly said to me, "No, we're not moving." I was built up to have an argument but he just said, no it's immaculate, we're not moving.*'

So the new chairman astonished the supporters, and probably many of his own staff, by revealing that City would stay at Boothferry Park until the new ground was built. However, Cooper knew that it may have only been a temporary stay of execution and he was thankful that the Kwiksave lease effectively scuppered any hopes Lloyd may have had over a quick sale of the Boothferry Park site. He adds: '*When David Lloyd took over he divided Boothferry Park into two. He divided the ground into one company that he owned and the car park, supermarket, offices, gymnasium, training pitch and 268 North Road were in another company.*

'*The lease for Kwik Save came about in 1982 when the North Stand was demolished and the Jacksons supermarket was built. That rightly or wrongly gave the tenants a 125-year lease and it didn't take a lawyer to work out that we were only 13-14 years down the line and I know that David Lloyd knew this because I handed a copy of that contract to his advisors in advance. I just feel that despite the lease, certain people thought that they could just railroad through that with the view that Kwiksave was just a second-rate supermarket company and it would just crumble.*

'*What they may not have realised was that at that time, in the mid-Nineties, the Kwik Save store at Boothferry Park was their second biggest productive store in the whole of the old Humberside county, so they were not going to go without a fight. David Lloyd even put somebody on the doors, counting people in to check what they were saying. They offered to move for £4m but it was rejected and undoubtedly Kwiksave helped to keep Boothferry Park where it was.'*

City lost the Notts County game 3-0 and the start to the season was not what most supporters were expecting or hoping for. The football may have been prettier than in Dolan's time but it was no more effective. The September saw the club continue to do badly on the field, though a 7-4 victory over Jan Molby's Swansea lightened the mood.

Whilst the club were doing badly on the field, settling just off the bottom of the table, there were the beginnings of signs that behind the scenes, all was not well. Ian McMahon left his post as chief executive almost as quickly as he'd arrived to be replaced by Michael Appleton. Nigel Kaye left shortly afterwards and Tim Wilby, who arrived in such a blaze of publicity, was quietly shunted off to Australia in the dark of night to leave David Lloyd as chairman of the club.

Jeff Radcliffe was another departure in a sad end to a long and distinguished career with the club. Radcliffe says: *'I didn't want to leave, I was hoping that I'd ride out the storm and come out the other end but they started to transfer a lot of my stuff over to the Boulevard. It came to a head when we were playing Cardiff one day and I had a big piece of rehabilitation equipment for people who had leg injuries. I came back from Cardiff and it wasn't in the dressing room. I asked Mark the groundsman and he said as soon as I'd left, a lorry came, loaded it up and took it to the Boulevard. So I went storming off to see Appleton who was the chief exec and asked what was going on.*

'He said that Mark McGurn, who was the fitness coach, was going to be in charge of all rehabilitation and he was working from the Boulevard. He had no medical knowledge and couldn't deal with somebody who'd had a cruciate injury. I was quite willing for this guy to take over once a player had started running, fitness work is fine, but without the medical side you haven't got a clue. So I walked out, knowing that they didn't want me. I couldn't work in an environment like that.'

To those staff who had stayed with the club, it was a time of great upheaval. The club was now completely unrecognisable

LOOK BACK IN AMBER

from the time under the chairmanship of Martin Fish. The only similarities were the league position, still towards the bottom of the Football League. Rob Smith says: '*It was a shambles on the pitch and a shambles off the pitch in many ways. They moved in a lot of their outside people to Boothferry Park and a lot of the existing staff apart from the ticket office were moved to the Boulevard. You could see slowly what was happening as there were better corporate facilities there and quite a lot of the staff from the rugby club worked at Hull City games in the bars etc.*

'*Though fans were worried I personally never thought that we would be moved lock stock and barrel to the Boulevard which maybe is why I stuck it out. Whatever masterplan David Lloyd had, things were starting to crumble early on with people who he had appointed into senior positions leaving. There seemed to be no stability during that time so we were probably finding out more about what was happening from people on the outside looking in, who by that time were opposed to David Lloyd's plans.*'

Smith was still employed at the club but spent very little time at Boothferry Park and he acknowledges now that it was probably the lowest time in the club's history, not least because the heart of the club was practically being ripped out by those now in charge: '*David Lloyd's time was soul destroying purely because I had been at the club 10 years and I saw the history of the club slowly destroyed by people who didn't really give a damn about the club. I was at the Boulevard for the best part of a year, so I couldn't really keep an eye on things that were happening at Boothferry Park but, unbeknown to us, they were literally throwing out the club's history into skips.*

'*Anything that was associated with the club's past was chucked out. There was a skip in the car park and I've got some programme binders on the floor which were rescued from the skip. There were others which ended up in other people's hands and they resurfaced at the auction recently. We couldn't say they were ours because we couldn't prove it but it was items from the club's history including programmes which went back to the beginning of Boothferry Park.*'

176

LOCK-OUTS

Events on the pitch were not much better. Doncaster Rovers ensured that City were never in serious risk of going out of the league but one of the few Rovers victories that season was at Belle Vue against City in one of the worst ever displays by a side in amber and black. The City fans sang 'You're not fit to wear the shirt' and, although it was the Doncaster fans who went onto the pitch to protest that day, it was becoming apparent to the supporters that City had many problems of their own and the hopes and optimism which greeted Lloyd and Hateley the previous July had long since dissolved.

The depressing Doncaster game was the low point of a poor season and a handful of improved performances lifted the spirits a little, but City still finished third from bottom of the Third Division, the lowest position in their history. City had picked up only five points from 23 away games and suffered the shame of being knocked out of the FA Cup by non-league Hednesford Town, the first time that a non-league club had beaten City in the competition. Warren Joyce was player of the year having come to Boothferry Park from Burnley in July 1996 after having successful loan spells at the club.

Despite the team having such a poor season, the average attendance at Boothferry Park was over 4,600, the third highest in the division, compared to 3,400 in the previous season.

Once the season had ended Hateley said that he knew after one week of training in Hull that it would be difficult to stay up. He said that there were only about half a dozen players of the standard that he needed to get the club out of the league and he had indeed put nine players on the transfer list within two months. Hateley said that the following season would be the time to judge him so he had a busy summer ahead to attempt to mould the team into one he felt capable of challenging in the top half of the league. One player they were going to have to do without was Duane Darby. The striker didn't want to leave the club and had almost agreed a new deal with Mark Hateley but chief executive Michael Appleton got involved and Darby was forced out of the club. He went to Notts County but ruptured his Achilles within a few weeks and towards the end of his time at

Nottingham he came back to Boothferry Park on loan before joining Rushden and Shrewsbury.

Though the jury was out on Hateley's managerial talents, most City fans were patient during that season with both Lloyd and Hateley. Most felt that Lloyd was still putting the club back into shape after the mess he inherited and Hateley received the same benefit of the doubt, with most of the players in the team having been inherited from Terry Dolan's time.

Jeff Radcliffe, however, wasn't impressed with the new manager or indeed the whole regime. He says: *'Mark Hateley was an arrogant prat who was just in it for the money. It's sickening when you think he was there about two years and got about £700,000 as a pay-off and I was there 25 years and got bugger all and that rankled. He just didn't care. None of them did, I'd swing for Appleton if I ever saw him again.*

'You'd very rarely see Lloyd, just on match days, Appleton was his henchman and Calam was also involved. I tried to avoid them at all costs. I tried initially to just get on with my job and keep my head down because you could tell it was a horrible time and you didn't want to be in their company.'

However, by the start of the 1998-99 season supporters were looking for signs that real progress was showing through on and off the pitch. Even a mid-table finish would have been progress after the total disappointment of what they had put up with over the past few years. With more pace and a greater physical presence in the side, to add some steel to the skill that was apparent in some of the players, that could have been achieved.

Hateley's shopping list included two defenders, two midfielders, two strikers and a new goalkeeper if Scott Thompson managed to secure a club in Scotland. He was given a budget believed to be in the region of £250,000 but it was reported that if David Lloyd managed to secure a deal with Kwik Save to move the supermarket from Boothferry Park, thus freeing the site for sale, more money would be given to the manager.

Season 1998-99

With City only surviving relegation the season before due to a desperate Doncaster Rovers, who had relegation tied up well before the end of the season, it was hoped that fans had seen the one and only time that City were to flirt with relegation from the Football League.

However, the 1998-99 season saw City, once again, struggling at the bottom. The Tigers scored one of the earliest goals of the season with David D'Auria putting us one-up at Rotherham in the first game but we were to lose the game 3-1 and were only two off the bottom by the time of the first win when we beat Peterborough at home.

Two further defeats followed but a 2-1 victory over Rochdale at Boothferry Park took us up to the dizzy heights of eighteenth place. Five defeats in a row followed and by the time of our next win, at Scarborough, the Tigers were bottom of the table and heading for the Conference unless the season could be turned around quickly. Changes in the boardroom and in the dug-out had to be made yet again if the club had any hope of survival and, once again, the papers were full of 'interested parties' eager to walk into Boothferry Park and take the club off Lloyd's hands.

Lloyd himself was still threatening to sell Boothferry Park and move City to the Boulevard, though this time talk about a new super-stadium was sketchy at best. Bryan Calam, supporting the move, argued that fans do not support a ground, aptly summing up why he and the supporters never exactly saw eye to eye. It was beginning to dawn on supporters that, in their own way, the Lloyd/Wilby takeover, so hailed a year earlier, was threatening to become an even bigger disaster for the club.

As the team remained rooted to the bottom of the table, so protests against Lloyd's regime and his intention on a move to the Boulevard grew. Relations between Lloyd and the fans reached a new low when tennis balls were thrown onto the pitch during a League Cup tie against Bolton Wanderers in protest over the Boulevard plans.

LOOK BACK IN AMBER

The Boulevard move was also threatening takeover talks. Tom Belton, the former chairman of Scunthorpe United, had made clear his interest in Hull City and he met Calam and Michael Appleton to make a bid for the club, stating that he was backed by wealthy businessmen who wanted to take over control at Boothferry Park. He pledged to keep the club at Boothferry but said that he would not be interested in buying the club if Lloyd went ahead with his proposal to move the club to the Boulevard.

By the October of 1998 Lloyd went a stage further and announced to the media that unless a new buyer could be found for Hull City he would close the club down. In an incredible interview on national radio, Lloyd accused the city of being in the Dark Ages and spoke of his plans to move the club to the Boulevard. He said: *'I would have wanted to try and merge the two clubs (City and Hull Sharks), sell the ground and move into a stadium like the Reebok Stadium. The Boothferry Park fans have actually come to me, I've met them, they said they do not want that, they do not want this, they want to stay at Boothferry Park which is falling down.'*

In the radio interview he also managed to anger Mark Hateley by stating that the City manager was on £250,000 a year and that his and Billy Kirkwood's salary accounted for one third of City's wage bill. Hateley responded by saying that the chairman's claim was 'ludicrous' but Lloyd insisted that the manager's basic salary was £150,000 and had a series of 'perks' written into his contract including a payment of £1,000 a match, an enhanced pension scheme, a car and a house which Lloyd claimed he had bought for Hateley and was worth £250,000.

According to Martin Fish, Lloyd's outburst was an indication that City's owner didn't have the moral fibre to stay with the job until the end. Fish claims that, although unpopular, he stayed with the club, making decisions which, although supporters may not have liked, at least ensured the survival of the club whereas Lloyd was making decisions which put the club's future in jeopardy.

Fish adds: *'What I had to put up with, David Lloyd couldn't stand in the end. AGMs were frightening experiences. Towards the end we had an AGM in the gym which was incredible and when David Lloyd had one like that he walked out, he couldn't stand it.*

180

LOCK-OUTS

That was the problem. David Lloyd didn't have the character to stand up to it all even though he had the money.'

It was make or break time at City. Belton was still interested, but only if City were to remain at Boothferry Park. The club was stranded at the foot of the table looking likely to be relegated from the Football League and there was the increasing likelihood of City playing host to the likes of Morecambe and Forest Green Rovers at the Boulevard the following August.

Belton had an official bid for City rejected in September but it appeared that Lloyd was keener to sell as a result of the protests against him, which reached a head at the Bolton game. The day after the game he instructed Michael Appleton to contact the consortium and accept the offer. This was once again rejected due to a change in the method and timescale of payment, according to Appleton but the deal remained on the timetable and it was becoming more likely that Lloyd would soon be leaving Hull City.

The *Hull Daily Mail* of October 19 reported that Irish businessman Kevin Phelan was set to take over the club from David Lloyd, promising £100,000 of funds to go towards team strengthening. A spokesman for Phelan's firm Gameplan International, said: *'I can confirm that the heads of terms agreement between David Lloyd and Gameplan International have been passed off and that contracts will be exchanged today which will mean the club is in new hands.'*

The news of Phelan's interest came at the same time as former chairman Don Robinson declared his interest in returning to the club and at one stage claimed that he was on the verge of buying the club once again, saying that the deal had reached an advanced stage with accountants checking over the figures. He later said that after looking at the figures he decided to pull out but expressed the hope that whoever took over would keep the club at Boothferry Park and not move the club lock stock and barrel to the Boulevard.

Robinson explained: *'Under Lloyd we nearly bought the club but I met his people and I didn't like the way they wanted it to work out. Also, I had a triple by-pass so I couldn't have done it anyway. I wanted to do my bit to help the club because I didn't like to see it slipping. If I get involved, I get involved 100% but I wouldn't have been able to and thankfully Adam Pearson came in, got the finance in and things have gone right ever since.'*

Eventually, the news was announced that a takeover had been agreed with a consortium led by Tom Belton. We didn't know who was behind him, only that there were others in the consortium. We weren't to rid the city of Lloyd altogether though as he was to keep hold of Boothferry Park and eventually become the 'landlord from hell'.

Rob Smith, one of the few to survive the Lloyd influenced 'cull' at Boothferry Park, remembers his first meeting with the new boss: *'Tom came in with a purely football background, he had experience from Scunthorpe, but there was a fall-out at boardroom level and he was forced out. We all got brought together and were summoned to Boothferry Park and assembled in the shop. There were Hull FC staff and Hull City staff all together and Tom came in, the knight in shining armour! He had a charm and a very easy-going approach, waltzed in with a fag in his mouth and said who he was. He said that nobody need worry, everything was going to be fine.*

'You couldn't help but like Tom. He was media friendly, talked a good game and seemed to trust everybody and let them get on with their jobs. There was no real pressure from him at all, he was quite happy with a smoke and going to the pub to meet the supporters. Unfortunately I think he paid the price for that attitude later on when he fell out with the people behind the consortium. At the time we didn't really know who was behind it, we just thought that Tom was the money man and it was going to be his club.

'Slowly, more and more people moved over from other clubs, especially the Sheffield connection. We didn't know who Nick Buchanan was, we'd probably seen him in the office, but we didn't know who he was and we didn't know some of the businessmen who he brought in at the same time. Obviously they had all got together to form this consortium and they all had their roles in the running of the club, but it wasn't clear to us for a fortnight or so who was who and who was doing what.'

By this time City had already bade farewell to Billy Kirkwood, Hateley's assistant, who was doubtless happy to escape the scene and accept the position as assistant manager at St Johnstone before his reputation could take any further punishment. Hateley appointed his most senior player, Warren Joyce, as his new assistant.

However, Hateley was not to last much longer and one of Tom Belton's first acts was to dispense with the services of the manager. Hateley had gone to the media to say that he was willing to take a pay cut in order to stay with the club but, as Lloyd had made clear to everyone, he was on an extortionate contract and, with the Tigers stranded at the foot of the table, he had to go.

One could see the reasons why Wilby went for Hateley at the time. He had the right image and City fans were desperate for a 'name' after the Fish/Dolan time, which seemed so grey and lifeless. However, the foundations, on and off the field, were built on sand. He had inherited a side which finished 17th in the Third Division under Dolan, and had spent just £25,000 to try and turn water into wine. Some of his acquisitions worked to some degree, such as McGinty, while others such as Thompson and Gage plainly didn't. The team as a whole certainly didn't work and without a change in manager, City would almost certainly have gone down.

Rob Smith says of Hateley's time as manager: '*Mark became a good friend but was not clued up at all as a manager and had no respect for the players. I don't think he had any intention of playing games for us, he wasn't fit enough. They went for a high profile name to try and get bums on seats. It worked initially with 2,500 going to Mansfield for the first game but it didn't last very long. Some of the players came with good backgrounds and showed individual bits of skill but collectively as a team it didn't gel.*'

In the days following Hateley's departure, Neil Warnock, Mick Wadsworth, John Ward and Colin Addison were seen as the prime candidates to take up the considerable challenge which existed at Boothferry Park. All recognised managers of some reputation, they would all arguably have been more popular than Warren Joyce who was still seen by supporters as one of Dolan's men who had criticised the fans during the darkest days of Dolan's reign. He also worsened his case by famously celebrating a goal in front of an empty East Stand, a gesture forgotten by few City fans. However, Joyce was the assistant manager so was in prime position to fill the vacancy when Hateley left.

LOOK BACK IN AMBER

So, within hours of City losing 2-0 at home to Brighton, Joyce was installed as caretaker-manager and his first act was to bring in John McGovern, a long-time friend, as his assistant. The pair had met whilst at Bolton Wanderers when McGovern gave Joyce his first taste of league football.

Joyce's bid to land the job on a permanent basis was hardly strengthened by just one win in his first six league games to see City further stranded at the bottom of the table. However, the new manager did see his team go on something of a cup run. City overcame Salisbury City 2-0 with goals from Rioch and McGinty to be faced with the daunting prospect of playing Luton Town away in round two.

Luton were going well towards the top of the Second Division and with City's form being atrocious, were strong favourites to progress through to the next round. City were hampered further by being without nine first team regulars. Ben Morley put City ahead with a super goal but Luton equalised through Steve Davis and looked the more likely to get a winner. However, it was the Tigers who scored a second when a free-kick in the Luton box saw Rob Dewhurst get above his marker to nod the ball home, to the delight of the City fans in the seats behind the goal.

As a reward for beating Luton, City were through to the third round of the FA Cup and got a plum draw, away at Premiership Aston Villa. The two clubs had moved in very different circles since City last played them on New Year's Day 1988. That game saw Villa win 5-0 and the end of the season saw Villa promoted to the old First Division, while City hung around a couple more years before the inevitable relegation and the start of a rapid descent.

So, at the time of the game there were a full four divisions separating the sides, Villa were top of the Premiership and City bottom of the Third Division. Despite this, the *Hull Daily Mail's* coverage grated, with the paper producing a special issue on the game, going to town on the top v bottom clash. City should have been playing the likes of Aston Villa every week so few City fans were impressed that the local paper appeared to consider us a minnow even if circumstances dictated that we were for this game. Villa comfortably won the game 3-0 but the City fans who went to

LOCK-OUTS

Villa Park were not too distraught as there were far more important battles ahead.

Staying in the league was the priority and results after the Villa game started to improve. City's next five league games saw three wins and two draws claw back what had been a six-point deficit at the bottom of the table and the final result of that five-game sequence, a fine win away at Brentford, saw the Tigers off the bottom for the first time since September.

The new Joyce/McGovern team was taking shape and the pair had signed virtually a new team within a few weeks of taking over. Andy Oakes took over in goal, Steve Swales and Garreth Williams were new wing-backs, Justin Whittle, Jason Perry and John Whitney came in to the centre of defence, Gary Brabin strengthened the midfield and Colin Alcide did likewise up front. City had spent a quarter of a million on transfer fees whilst other players came in on loan.

By April, City had been beaten just twice in 18 games, promotion form if repeated throughout the season, and safety was within sight. A gate recorded as 14,000, though there were probably many more inside the ground, saw City draw 1-1 with closest challengers Scarborough, but City ensured safety with a draw at promotion-chasing Cardiff and a win over Exeter.

Despite other struggling teams continuing to pick up points, City had made survival certain with two games to go and ensured a carnival atmosphere at the last home game of the season, against Torquay. Joyce and McGovern were justly rewarded with three-year contracts and chairman Tom Belton, still the public face of the consortium, was given a rousing ovation before the game and was even named supporter of the year by the official supporters' club.

Belton said it had been hard work turning the club around but that he and the other directors had seen the enormous potential for a successful football club in Hull. As things started going right on the field, the new board began to emerge from the shadows. Previously the name Nick Buchanan had just been a name in the programme under that of Belton's but he was soon to take centre stage.

Rob Smith says: '*The first time I met Nick Buchanan was an away cup game, I think at Hayes or somewhere down south, and he was instantly likeable. The staff that came in, mainly from Sheffield United, came with a lot of experience and were highly regarded within football, Dave Capper, Andy Daykin, people like that. Things looked really good and suddenly we had a very professional, commercial outfit.*

'They all came with such passion for football. I don't think they knew what they were doing, but they made Hull City their lives for a short period. I may get funny looks in the street for saying that but working so closely with them, socialising with them, we didn't ever dream that anything suspect would ever rear its head. Obviously Stephen Hinchcliffe brought with him some baggage but the people they brought in were all well thought of in football circles.'

It seemed that the new board could do no wrong although one unpopular change came when they tried to play around with the club badge. Again, Rob Smith had some sympathy for them in this regard.

'As daft as it seemed, the club never had a trademarked badge of identity, it was a mis-match of a Tiger's head. If you look through the old programmes there were some different variations on the Tiger's head theme although there was one which was settled on, which we have gone back to in recent years. So I think what the new people at the time did was to try and create a new identity. Just as Adam did when he came in, although he wanted to keep with tradition.

'Unfortunately they didn't use my experience of the club or knowledge of the club to do that. I fought as best I could against it but without making any inroads. I think it was Hinchcliffe's son who was studying art, so to hurt the feelings of a gentleman who was quite involved with the club, by saying, "That's a load of crap!" wasn't in my best interests at the time. We did tweak and develop it a little bit but unfortunately it was too late and it was a case of swallow your pride and get on with it.

'It still haunts us to this day as it has a habit of reappearing every now and again in certain forms. Although it was a bloody awful looking thing, at least it showed they tried to get something that was definitely Hull City and that could be used on merchandise.'

LOCK-OUTS

It was testament to the new optimism around Boothferry Park that the badge should be one of the more contentious issues at the time. We had a popular chairman and a manager who, though unpopular at the time of his appointment, had performed miracles to keep City in the Football League. A traumatic season had ended with the Tigers still intact and looking forward to, what supporters hoped, would be a promotion campaign the following season.

Season 1999-2000

Tom Belton's arrival at the club signalled a return to the club by John Cooper who was one of many who left under David Lloyd's time at the club: '*I came back to the club, ironically through Martin Fish, in that I received a phone call from Tom Belton who said that he had been talking to Martin and that he had a problem which Martin thought I may be able to help with. I think that Tom nearly joined the City board at some time in the Nineties when Martin Fish was chairman.*

'*The problem was that at the beginning of the 1999-2000 season they had a real job to try and get a safety certificate for the ground to be used for the pre-season friendlies and the first game of the season. We started work to get the South Stand useable and then I put it to them that I would work on the North Stand once the season was underway. For the first game against Lincoln we had both of these stands in use and Boothferry Park had a capacity of 9,000, though we had lost the whole of the East Stand.*'

With the Kempton closed, the Lincoln game was made all-ticket and it was assumed that many of the home games would have to be designated this way because of the limited capacity. This was assuming that the team played their part by getting into the top half of the table. The 1999-2000 season saw City with heightened expectations due to the previous 'great escape' season and the seemingly quality purchases that the new board allowed Warren Joyce to make.

LOOK BACK IN AMBER

That new board no longer included Tom Belton who had been sacked by the consortium with Nick Buchanan taking over as City chairman. The board claimed that Belton was not a 'team player' and that Hateley would still have been at the club if it had been left to him. However, to most City fans he did not get the supporter of the year award for nothing and his role in the great escape would never be forgotten.

Likewise, Warren Joyce had plenty of goodwill in the tank following his efforts the previous season, but, due to the promotion form since he took over, City fans did not expect another season nearer the bottom than the top of the division. The Hinchcliffe/Buchanan board had a five-year plan to get the club into the First Division and nobody wanted to 'hang around' in the Third Division much longer.

Lee, Bracey, John Eyre, Steve Harper, Jason Harris, Steve Morgan, John Schofield and Jamie Wood were all brought in to aid the Tigers' promotion push but the team again got off to a poor start.

City lost to Exeter in the opening game of the new season in which the Tigers outplayed Exeter for most of the first half but were unable to finish with Colin Alcide, Jason Harris and David Brown all missing good opportunities to get the campaign off to a good start. Despite the pressure, City were unable to get the goal they needed and the hosts inevitably took the game with a fluke late on.

By the end of August, City were 22nd in the table, having scored just three goals and had picked up a solitary point. Despite beating Rotherham to progress to the second round of the Worthington Cup, it was hardly the exciting new start which the fans had expected.

September was a better month with a four match unbeaten run featuring victories against Chester, Torquay and Swansea but by then attendances had already started to fall and only cup ties ensured that financial losses did not accrue too heavily. The reward for beating Rotherham was a tie against Liverpool over two legs. The first leg, televised live, was at Boothferry Park but City went down to a 5-1 defeat and though the second leg was 2-2 for a time, Liverpool scored twice more to make it a 9-3 aggregate win for the Premiership side.

LOCK-OUTS

By Christmas, City were still in the bottom half of the table and though the arrival of Theodore Whitmore and Ian Goodison from Jamaica ensured that City made the headlines, with both showing their class, they did not spark a dramatic revival in the team's fortunes.

Nick Culkin, a classy keeper, played his part in another mini-revival but City remained stranded in the lower half of the table, never in danger of going down, but not remotely consistent enough, or good enough, to force their way into the top half.

The defence was strong with Whittle continuing to excel alongside Ian Goodison and the midfield offered plenty of protection, but there was a lack of creativity in the side with the exception of Theo Whitmore who, despite looking far too good for the division in some games, flattered to deceive in many others.

John Eyre showed his class up front, though he suffered from a lack of service and the lack of a regular partner. Gary Bradshaw had plenty of promise and David Brown also showed glimpses of class but, if ever we needed Chris Chilton back on the coaching staff, it was surely now with young strikers eager to learn.

The closing weeks of the season saw plenty of draws followed by a three-game winning streak to send City up to 14th place, but by that time Warren Joyce and John McGovern had left Boothferry Park. The board, impatient for success, had expected a promotion push and were disappointed to see City in the bottom half of the division for practically the whole season. With fans similarly impatient to see the side climbing the table, they decided to dispense with the services of Warren Joyce.

Nick Buchanan said: *'The board feels that its objective of achieving First Division status at the earliest opportunity will be best achieved by the appointment of an experienced manager with a proven track record and steps will be taken to ensure that such an appointment is made as soon as possible.'*

Responding to the sacking, John McGovern said: *'Nothing surprises me in football because I have been in the game for a long time so I will just have to accept the decision and get on with things.'*

Though the sackings of Joyce and McGovern were a shock and Joyce had retained much of the goodwill he had built up the previous season, most supporters agreed with the decision as another season of under-achievement in the bottom division reached its climax. The board did not waste any time in appointing his successor either and that was to be another surprise. Brian Little, the ex-Aston Villa boss, was reported to be heading a consortium of businessmen who were ready to take control of the club and were considering buying a 65% stake which would mean Buchanan and Hinchcliffe selling their shares. There was to be no new consortium taking control but Little admitted being interested in the job and a couple of days later, appeared before the press with the obligatory black and amber scarf held up above his head.

Despite a less than successful time at Stoke and West Brom, memories of him at Aston Villa were still fresh in the minds and when his arrival was confirmed he was City's highest profile appointment arguably since Terry Neill. He also had a proven track record, perhaps the first City appointment since Cliff Britton to do so and the supporters were reassured that City now had an experienced manager who had shown himself capable of getting teams promoted before, who also knew his way through the divisions.

Little's first game was City's last of the 1999-2000 season and Hartlepool came to Boothferry Park needing the points to secure a play-off place. They gained them, winning the game 3-0, and the Tigers' new manager knew exactly the job he had on his hands as City failed to make a game of it.

City went into the close season hopeful that, with Little's experience, some better quality signings would come to City and hopefully, at last, take the club forward. Meanwhile, in May 2000, as the season was coming to an end, it was announced that work was being planned on a £36m community stadium for the city with the ground - which would be situated at the Circle, adjacent to the site of City's original Anlaby Road ground - being shared by the Tigers and Hull FC.

A planning application was intended to be submitted with work due to start in early 2001. The major features included an all-seater stadium with the capacity between 25,000-30,000, an indoor sports arena with a 3,000 capacity, a new rail halt at Argyle Street, all weather sports pitches and a major sports and leisure retail store.

LOCK-OUTS

It was exciting news but there had been plans before and David Lloyd's arrival in the city was still fresh in the memory. The priority therefore was to stay at Boothferry Park until it was built and the City board, while welcoming the proposals, were guarded, leaving the way open for a decision to stay at Boothferry Park if desired.

The board had matters of their own to sort out as financial problems were mounting up and Lloyd's patience with the club was beginning to run out. A few weeks previously, City had to settle an outstanding tax debt of £40,000 despite selling Adam Bolder to Derby County for £90,000. The majority of that money had to be used to pay the players' wages as the first team squad had threatened strike action after several players' pay cheques bounced.

Losses at this time were about £15,000 a week and to make matters worse, officials from the Football Association were studying financial documents from the club dating back more than 12 months as part of their investigation into the running of Hull City. Nick Buchanan insisted that the club had nothing to hide but the club were fined £2,500 by the FA for failing to assist the investigation. The club were also the subject of a transfer embargo.

Worse was to come however as on May 24, David Lloyd repossessed the ground and instructed bailiffs to recover debts of £103,000 from the club. He claimed that he was owed the money in unpaid rent. A team of debt collectors visited the club and locked the premises, leaving staff unable to get into the ground. Buchanan was fuming and said that he had not been given any warning from Lloyd that the lockout would occur.

He added: '*We were given no notification that this was going to happen and I'm totally gobsmacked by the whole incident. I think what David Lloyd has done is totally unjust. I don't see any reason why we couldn't have sat round the table and discussed it like mature adults.*'

A team of security guards patrolled the ground whilst staff arriving for work were greeted by signs declaring 'warning, no entry'. Lloyd was also preparing to serve a winding up order on the club's directors and was thought to have had offers from businessmen who were interested in buying the ground. Lloyd said:

'*I have nothing against the club or the supporters, it is simply the case that I have no confidence in the directors of Hull City paying me what I am owed.*'

Being summer, the grass was growing untreated and essential maintenance work was not being done in preparation for the new season. John Cooper was completely in the hands of the directors, waiting for them to give him the all-clear to get back in and try to limit any damage done to the pitch and the stadium by neglect.

John Cooper said: '*I managed on the Saturday morning, after discussions with the board of directors, to get what I believed would be secure entry to the ground on the Saturday, two days after David Lloyd locked us out. The directors gave me the paperwork but the only area I was going to get access to were the offices, not the stadium, and that was to generate money. They weren't bothered about the stadium itself.*

'*I spoke to the press and said I didn't have the right keys, used all sorts of excuses while inwardly I was seething, I felt used. We got the ticket office working, I did press interviews, went home and then spoke to a few people by telephone and let them know in no uncertain terms what I thought about their antics. Their excuse was that it was the eleventh hour and they could not get the paperwork through. One director said to me about the pitch when we got back in, "Oh, it's not as bad as you said it was." It was typical of their attitude to the ground.*'

Season 2000-2001

After a traumatic summer, City began the 2000-2001 season having been able to sign only David Brightwell, Phil Brumwell and Lee Philpott as soon as the transfer embargo ended, although Clint Marcelle and Paul Musselwhite came in soon after the season started. Little's skills in management were clearly having an effect on the players though as even in the first game of the season, which saw City lose 3-1 to Blackpool, City played well and the score was no reflection on the game.

LOCK-OUTS

However, after nine games we had only won once and were back in the bottom half, though things looked up with a good win over promotion-chasing Cardiff. Though the team were way off the promotion places, there was hope as the Tigers were beginning to look a well-organised team with Eyre starting to look the part in attack, aided by Marcelle with Musselwhite boosting the defence. City began to climb the table and if the off-field problems could be resolved and Little given the resources that the board had provided for Joyce at the beginning of the previous season, a promotion challenge could be on the cards.

Little was playing Goodison in his rightful position in the centre of defence and his partnership with Justin Whittle was becoming one of the strongest in the division whilst Mark Greaves, though out of position in midfield, was doing a good enough job to keep Gary Brabin out of the side.

Also in midfield, Theodore Whitmore was in great form and was making such an impact that he was the subject of transfer speculation with Aberdeen and Nottingham Forest reported to be interested. A victory over Darlington pushed City up to ninth position, the highest of the season so far.

Problems off the field mounted though as the Inland Revenue chased £103,000 that City owed and the club were given 28 days in which to pay or face a winding-up order. Nick Buchanan was forced to deny that City were £1.5m in the red and that he may have to sell his controlling interest in the club but at a packed fans' forum, the chairman finally admitted that City were in severe financial trouble. The club were bringing in much less than anticipated at the gate and had a crippling wage bill.

Buchanan said that wages would have to be slashed by £35,000 a month in order to avoid financial disaster as part of new proposals aimed at making the club financially viable on gates of just 5,000.

The situation reached breaking point around New Year 2001. Rob Smith was, by this time, one of the more experienced members of staff at the club. He said: *'We were due to play Blackpool at home on New Year's Day and it got snowed off and that game almost signed and sealed the club's fate from what I heard around the club. The gate money lost from that game was probably the time when Buchanan and others at board level realised that the game was up and they now had no more money to keep the club afloat forcing it to go into administration.'*

John Cooper added: '*The thing that blew everything out of the water was the postponed game. We were feeding hand to mouth and down at the stadium we were concerned about a frozen pitch because we needed the gate money to pay the staff. If a game is postponed on an event day you still have to pay the caterers, programme sellers, certain staff etc, so it was vital to get the game on.*

'The ref came in and I took him to the South Stand end first because that was the best end. He thought it was 60:40 in favour of the game taking place. I gave him a Met Office forecast and I felt we would have got the game on. The thing was that one of his linesmen came onto the pitch and didn't have the correct footwear for a pitch that was still semi-frozen. He managed to convince the referee that it was dangerous for the players so the game was postponed and the following week, the club went into administration.'

Though the club continued to operate, the Tigers players and staff were going unpaid and on February 3 City beat Cheltenham 1-0 with the three points lifting City to tenth in the league, but within 72 hours Buchanan had finally stepped aside as City chairman and handed over control of the club to administrators Kroll, Buchler and Phillips. The club were more than £1.5m in debt and had been served with a winding up order in the High Court due to an unpaid tax bill.

Nick Buchanan said: '*I always said I would resign from the club if I felt I was holding them back and I've felt this week that I've been a handicap to them rather than a help. I also did it because I want the club to have a future and I feel the only way for that to happen is for me to step aside and let someone else come in. I am passionate about Hull City and want them to survive.'*

To add considerable insult to injury, David Lloyd locked the club out of Boothferry Park after the club failed, once again, to pay the rent on the ground. This lock-out was different from the last one though as it was in the middle of the season and the club had fixtures to fulfil.

LOCK-OUTS

Rob Smith said: '*I found out about the lockout when we arrived at the ground. We arrived for work and press cameras had started to arrive. Word had spread but it pretty much happened overnight and was very underhand. We literally sat in our cars in the car park trying to look inconspicuous as the press roamed around.*

'*David Lloyd locked us out for unpaid rent but we still had a short period, still working with the Buchanan people before some of them were made redundant when the receivers came in. Those of us left used to make camp up at Fiveways pub, either just to sit and talk though some of us were able to get on with our work there. I was able to still do quite a bit of work from my car or from offices in Hull where people were good enough to put us up for a little while and stick a computer in front of us.*'

Lloyd said that if something wasn't done about the club's financial situation then it would simply lurch from crisis to crisis and under Buchanan and Hinchcliffe, City had reached the point where they couldn't continue trading and couldn't even get into the ground!

Rob Smith adds: '*There were times even before the lockout that we were travelling to games in cars, cramped up in little two-door coupes going up and down the motorway to games. It was like Sunday League but some of those players and staff at that time have become really good friends and it's always good to meet up with them again. We all used to go out together and there was no split between staff, management or players. In that period, whether people were due in at work or not, they came to support each other.*

'*The people who kept it together were Andy Daykin and Dave Capper, but their hands were tied as much as anybody's. So for the few days we took our directions from them. Then all of a sudden they were sacked and we were the only ones left but luckily we had some experience by then in all sorts of different roles.*

'*John Cooper was another who had made it his business to know how a football club runs, not just from the ground side but from the stadium and the office and everything. So us two and other people there at the time were able to run a football club in the intermediate period with the administrators and kept it going until Adam took control and I think we did a damn good job.*

LOOK BACK IN AMBER

'Despite the ground being locked, the players could still go and train because that was off-site. Brian Little was a great link man at the time because as prospective new owners came in, and obviously Adam was one of them, Brian was able to give us comfort in the fact that everything was going to be OK, because he had been approached and was seen as a major part of the plans.

'As manager he was able to try and persuade the players to stick with us and managed it although a couple had to go for personal reasons. They simply couldn't afford not to be paid and whilst it looked to others as though they jumped ship, it was their only option. Within two years most of those lads were out the game anyway, either working as labourers on building sites or just out the game.'

Many were linked with taking over the club with Hull FC, Mel Stein and Chris Waddle among the names being mentioned. There was talk of mystery Greeks, a consortium led by two American businessmen and the Tigers Co-operative, who were trying to raise the cash needed to buy the club.

City either had to get into Boothferry Park to fulfil the Leyton Orient fixture or ask the Football League to postpone the game. One solution came from south of the Humber as Grimsby Town vice-chairman Brian Huxford said that somebody with an association to City had been in touch with Grimsby to ask about the possibility of playing the match at their Blundell Park ground. He said they would be happy to help out but in the event the administrators managed to persuade Lloyd to open the gates and the match went ahead.

Rob Smith was one of the few remaining members of staff at this point: 'The next game was against Leyton Orient and we were still locked out of the ground. The remaining staff, about three or four of us, had to make a snap decision. We had a game on the Saturday and we had to back into Boothferry Park. John Cooper had his stadium to rectify, to get the grass right and you'll find that he did get in during this time to do some maintenance to the pitch. Though there were no armed guards on the doors, there were padlocks on the doors and the locks had been changed, but knowing the ground inside out as John did there was a way.

LOCK-OUTS

'Eventually, Lloyd relented and we were allowed in to complete the fixture. We worked literally around the clock for three days and did it by assuming these different roles. We got sponsors in, got the programme done and I remember hosting my first day in the sponsors' room. I'd never done it before but I'd seen Andy Daykin do it so I had to. I remember writing out a speech and reading it out in the bath the night before the game. I got there, knew everybody in the room and just made a complete bollocks of it really. I think though that everyone there appreciated that I had tried.

'So we put the game on, won the game and went on a winning run that took us through until Adam came and took us right into the play-offs. We could have all walked at that time, because I don't think we were getting paid and I married that year so money was tight. It was big news that the players didn't get paid but the staff didn't get paid either. I think we worked for five, six weeks without pay and then it started getting drip-fed through from the administrators in cloth bags, with change which had been collected at the gate.'

John Cooper adds: The second lockout was during the season and we knew that if David Lloyd was going to lock the football club out, the best time to do it would be on the eve of a game. So I hatched a plan to have people in the stadium with lights on and claim squatters' rights. There were two games in particular in which I know the bailiffs would have come in. So a little group of people, me included, would ensure that games would continue to be played on a Saturday afternoon at Boothferry Park.

After being let into Boothferry Park, promotion contenders Leyton Orient were beaten thanks to a goal from Rodney Rowe in front of almost 9,000 and a week later Rowe and Francis were on target in a 2-0 win at Shrewsbury. City followed these results up with two more wins, beating Mansfield and Barnet to climb up to eighth in the table, one place below the play-offs and despite the club being in administration and the players not being paid, City had a 100% record throughout February with five wins in a row, climbing from fourteenth to eighth, a record which deservedly won Brian Little the Manager of the Month award.

LOOK BACK IN AMBER

By March the players had still not been paid since the turn of the year and Brian Little was forced into cutting back on the number of training sessions as some of the players could not afford to put petrol in their cars to make the journey to the training field. Several squad members were tipped to move onto other clubs but in the end only Steve Harper, David Brightwell and Clint Marcelle moved. Little was also linked with a managerial vacancy at Portsmouth but chose to stay with the Tigers, despite also being without money for weeks.

Those who stayed with the Tigers were about to be rewarded as before the game against Brighton on March 10, creditors and shareholders agreed to back proposals for a rescue package funded by a mystery man. By the time City had grabbed a point away at Plymouth on March 13, the mystery man had been unveiled as former Leeds United commercial director Adam Pearson. He immediately won over the supporters and everyone at the club by paying the players and staff back-wages, one of several stipulations contained in a complicated takeover package.

With Pearson as chairman, a new era began for City and the Buchanan time ended in disgrace, though not everyone feels that their intentions were dishonourable. Rob Smith still retains an element of trust in the people he worked with at that time: '*I think they treated it more like a hobby rather than a business and they probably gambled that if everything had come off and we had had a good season, then whatever little investment they had put into the football club would have paid dividends. I don't think they threw a great deal at it, so that tells me it was more of a hobby, enjoyment for them rather than the business it is now.*

'*They were trying to get the club going in the right direction but I think, unfortunately, they didn't run out of steam or enthusiasm, they just ran out of cash and I'm never going to question that. I always got paid up until the administration/lockout time and the staff were always treated fairly, more so than under the David Lloyd regime.*

'*Though people say they nearly stripped the club, they weren't the first to have a go and fail, so in that case they shouldn't be made to look any worse or any different to some of the previous regimes who had come in and nearly destroyed the club. From the inside looking out they were as good as it got as a team of people, but from a supporter's view that will count for nothing as the club nearly suffered.*

'I was very relieved in some way that nothing ever did come to light. I'm sure there is a case to answer somewhere but I was never privy to the financial dealings of the club. I didn't need to be. We didn't know that things were particularly bad until the January, but I think there are one or two of us who would be very disappointed if anything was found. I'm not saying they were all pure, but until anything is proved I wouldn't change my opinion of them. If you talk to any of the staff who were around at that time, I don't think any of them would have a bad word. Whatever happened in the long run was good for the club because Adam came along and we got this new lease of life.'

However, John Cooper doesn't agree and said: *'I didn't feel they had the club at heart. I felt that we would never have seen a new stadium if they had continued to be in charge of the club. I was also afraid that we wouldn't have a football club, that's how I felt at the time.'*

It was a new era, we had had bright new eras on a regular basis since 1997 when David Lloyd took over but this one felt different. Pearson didn't have the arrogance of Lloyd or Wilby, appeared to have more ambition for the club than Tom Belton and didn't issue promises he felt he couldn't keep. With the new stadium by this time a reality, there was just a chance that this new era could be a good one.

The Tigers lost 3-0 at Brighton on March 10, just days before Pearson took over but it turned out to be the last defeat of the regular season with the team going on a 13-game unbeaten run. A glorious 3-1 defeat of leaders Chesterfield at Boothferry Park, with Ryan Williams starring for the visitors, virtually guaranteed that City would qualify for the end of season play-offs.

Rob Smith says of the takeover: *'When Adam came to the club he already knew a lot about it and more than anybody he lives and breathes it 24 hours a day. So he really does know the history of the club and is anxious not to destroy that, but he didn't want any links with the previous regime at all, be it in design of logo, in the chair he sat in, anything, for his own reasons. No reasons that he has tried to put over to us, the staff who were here under the old regime. He's never tried to separate us from that or warn us against speaking to anybody.'*

Cooper also feels that the new stadium, which was by now, with Lloyd out of the way, solidly back on the agenda, was in jeopardy with the board still in place: '*I know that the council were very edgy at the time. Tom Belton had left the club at this stage and I feel personally that Tom had been used by the consortium to get their hands on the football club. Once the club had been secured, he was surplus to requirements. The vibes around the city were that the new stadium was going to happen; we just had to ensure that the football club was totally behind it and that wasn't just releasing Boothferry Park. I just felt that the council felt very edgy about the directors of the club at the time. That all changed when Adam Pearson took over.'*

PART SEVEN

Back where we belong

Season 2001-2002

A brand new kit, new faces in the directors box, players making their City debuts, a boiling hot day and 2,000 travelling City fans going to cheer the Tigers on in the first game of a new season which would surely get the Tigers out of this dreadful division. Sound familiar?

This time though there was no big anti-climax on opening day. City were away at Exeter for the second time in three seasons and once again there had been an influx of new players in the summer. However, whereas those players had been Jason Harris, Lee Bracey, John Schofield and the like, in preparation for the 2001-2002 season City had spent about a million pounds on new players, breaking their transfer record to bring in Lawrie Dudfield from Leicester City. Matt Glennon, Nicky Mohan, Matt Bloomer, Mike Price, Andy Holt, Ben Petty, Ryan Williams, David Beresford, Julian Johnnson, David Lee, Lawrie Dudfield and Gary Alexander also came to the club and the substitutes for the Exeter game showed the quality City had throughout the squad compared to their rivals. Musselwhite, Whitmore, Price, Philpott and Rowe would have walked into most other teams in the division and Lee, Bloomer and Matthews did not even manage to get into the final 16.

City took the lead only to allow Exeter back into the game. However, this was a more talented City side than two years ago and the Tigers won the game 3-1 with record signing Lawrie Dudfield scoring the winning goal and securing a result that fired already raised expectations sky high.

Almost 11,000 packed into Boothferry Park for the first home game of the new season but they witnessed what was seen as a disappointing goalless draw with Plymouth. The Bank Holiday Monday saw Jan Molby's Kidderminster beaten 2-1 thanks to a last minute Alexander goal and Terry Dolan's York were thrashed 4-0 at Boothferry, with David Lee scoring an excellent goal from a free-kick.

BACK WHERE WE BELONG

City were hovering around the top three but the first seeds of doubt came when Mansfield deservedly beat second-placed City 4-2 at Field Mill, though at the time it was seen merely as a bad night at the office. City continued to stay in the top three or four but more doubts emerged about the team's capabilities on a humiliating night in the North East when the Tigers lost 4-0 to bottom of the table Hartlepool. The night also saw the first signs of a rift between manager and chairman when Brian Little let it be known that he wasn't best pleased by the comments that Adam Pearson had made after the defeat when he criticised what was a terrible City performance.

City then lost 2-1 at Lincoln City and though the team got back on track by beating Cheltenham 5-1 at home, another humiliating defeat, this time 3-0 away at Kidderminster, exposed the team's frailties in defence and the lack of support for Alexander.

Two more players were signed, Richard Sneekes and Jason Van Blerk, both with lots of league experience but a defeat at Plymouth led to City admitting that the title was beyond them and a revival in form was desperately needed if promotion was still to be achievable. Trips to York and Southend both brought defeats with the York away game a terrible experience in particular. Most City fans were incredulous at hearing that City's central midfield that night would be Whitmore and Sneekes and most of us prepared ourselves for defeat at that point. We weren't to be let down and York scored in the early stages of the game through Michael Proctor. They soon added a second and though Rodney Rowe reduced the arrears from the penalty spot, we never looked like getting back into the game after that, losing 2-1.

A 1-0 home defeat to Macclesfield on February 22nd heard Brian Little criticise his players for the first time that season. He sounded passionate that night about how the players had let him down and the season which had promised so much, was turning into another big let down, an even bigger let down considering how much money had been spent on new players. City were out of the top three and sliding further down the table but Brian Little would not have the opportunity of turning things around. The Macclesfield game was to prove his last in charge of the Tigers as the following week he was sacked and Billy Russell, the youth team coach was placed in temporary charge of the team.

Billy Russell did his own chances of getting the job on a permanent basis a lot of good when the team recreated some of their early season form in beating promotion hopefuls Mansfield 4-1, with Gary Bradshaw looking full of promise up front. However, City were struggling even to make the play-offs and three more defeats left them out of reach. This led to Pearson abandoning his plan to leave Russell in charge until the end of the season and he looked around for alternatives.

Jan Molby was not a name in the frame for the City job initially. Most people thought of Ronnie Moore being the favourite with other names such as Micky Adams, Mick Wadsworth, Ray Graydon and Brian Laws also being talked of. However, Molby had done well to get Kidderminster Harriers into the Football League and pushing towards a play-off place on extremely limited resources. With the City job available and his name eventually being mentioned, Molby resigned as manager of the Harriers and took up his new post as manager of Hull City in time for the final home game of the season.

The obligatory wave to the crowd by the new boss was followed by Molby and his new team being given a harsh football lesson by promoted Luton Town, who crushed the Tigers 4-0 and showed the new boss what he had let himself in for, as if he didn't already know. City looked to be desperately lacking in confidence and ideas and were a shambles of a team that afternoon. The new boss made it clear there would be changes during the summer and promised that the side would be fitter and more organised when the new season got underway.

Looking back on the 2001-2002 season, several mistakes were made before it began. Players like John Eyre were discarded despite them being responsible for a fantastic revival the season before, and the likes of Gary Brabin and John Whitney were also missed. The new team was probably more skilful but it was young and quiet, lacking a heart and badly needing leaders on the field. Also, several of the new signings just did not perform. Nicky Mohan played well on loan to the Tigers a few seasons before, but once on board, looked too slow to be an effective centre half and not a patch on the Whittle/Goodison partnership which had served City so well the previous campaign. Others such as David Lee and Matt Bloomer, despite being full of promise, were hardly given a chance in the first team.

However, as pre-season training started it was all change once again at Boothferry Park as the club prepared itself for the move to the new stadium. Molby had made a big impression and Adam Pearson had promised him money for more new players. Season ticket sales were also good going into the final season at Boothferry Park with the club due to move into the KC Stadium by Christmas.

Season 2002-03

The season which would see the Tigers move into a new home would surely also see the team move up a division. The big spending plan of the previous season had failed but with new manager Jan Molby having had a close season to reorganise, it was an optimistic Boothferry Park crowd that gathered for the opening day game against Southend.

Debutants Stuart Green and Stuart Elliott both scored for City but Southend got a last-minute equaliser to send the crowd home disappointed. However, there were positives to come out of the game. Another new signing, Ian Ashbee, though sent off towards the end of the game, looked a good signing and there was a new aggressive side to the Tigers which had been noticeably lacking the season before. Two away games, at Bristol Rovers and Exeter, saw a draw and a defeat. However, another disappointing draw, at home to Bury, was followed by the by now obligatory embarrassing performance at Hartlepool, with Molby sending City out in a 4-5-1 formation with Gary Alexander a very isolated figure up front.

City's very short purple patch under Molby saw the Tigers beat Cambridge away and Carlisle at home, but that was as good as it got under the new manager. A demoralising defeat at

LOOK BACK IN AMBER

Kidderminster, Molby's old club, led to a week of rumours, denied at the time, that Molby had offered to fall on his sword.

It was obvious that the manager was living on borrowed time and by the end of the week, as expected, Molby had gone, sacked by the club for a run of just two wins in 17 games with the club languishing in 18th place in the table. Pearson had acted quickly and he had a new manager in place by the time City next took to the field.

Peter Taylor was revealed as City's new manager and watched a side, picked by Billy Russell, beat Rochdale 3-0 at Boothferry Park. Taylor had just two months at Boothferry Park before the club made the move to the KC Stadium but still had time to make an impact with the highlight possibly being the 2-0 win over Scunthorpe in front of almost 12,000. The side played really well that day and fully deserved the win which came late in the game, with goals from on-loan Michael Branch and Gary Alexander.

14 December 2002 saw the last-ever first team game at Boothferry Park and an emotional day saw City lose to Darlington 1-0, despite having most of the game. A typically botched departure and though most supporters loved the ground, few were sad to be moving into the KC Stadium.

For Martin Fish, after so many years at Boothferry Park as supporter, director and chairman, the move to the KC was a poignant one. '*I was sad to leave Boothferry Park. In some respects I felt we could develop the ground. It would mean the gymnasium going and I thought the multi-storey car park would have to go because parking was going to be the problem at Boothferry Park, but that apart, the plan for the East Stand was not the end of it. I had the whole ground planned in stages. I put a lot of work into it and we could have got a lot of grants for it. I was sad because Boothferry Park is my place, but I can't fault the KC, you have to move on, progress has had to be made.*

'*Adam Pearson invited me to the first game at the KC Stadium and I got a good reaction there, especially from people at the Football League and Football Association. I thought they would have forgotten about me by then so that was nice. But it's the supporters who keep the feud going and I don't know how long this is going to go on for.'*

The Darlington game was a massive blow to City's receding chances of making the play-offs, though the Tigers showed what they could achieve by beating leaders Hartlepool 2-0 in the first league game to be played at the KC, on Boxing Day 2002.

Taylor rang the changes in personnel with Alexander, Bradshaw, Glennon, Johnnson, Price, Petty and Strong leaving the club and Fettis, Delaney, Burgess, Forrester, Webb and Melton coming in. However, City never looked likely to get into the play-offs with ninth place, early in January, being the highest position the team achieved that season.

Seasons 2003-04 & 2004-05

By the time of the Darlington game in the August of 2003, City had signed Andy Dawson, Richard Hinds, Jason Price, Alton Thelwell and Danny Allsopp whilst Stuart Green came back from Carlisle with a point to prove after walking out on City the season before.

We got off to a great start to the season, beating Darlington 4-1, and the encouraging thing was the way the team came back in the second half after Darlington equalised just before half-time, cancelling out Ben Burgess's early opener. The three second half goals, from Price, Thelwell and Allsopp, all came from debutants and with goals threatening to come from all areas of the pitch, we knew the season was going to be a good one.

It was. The forward line of Burgess and Allsopp with Price and Elliott on the wings was arguably the most exciting since Wagstaff, Chilton, Butler and Houghton. In some ways there is a neat symmetry as the team in 1970-71 was also full of goals. That side often promised much and gave the impression that First Division football would eventually be achieved. It didn't happen but maybe this time, with a new ground and in some respects a new 'crowd', it will.

We followed the Darlington victory with two defeats, a creditable loss in the Coca-Cola Cup away at Wigan before losing 2-1 to a thuggish Oxford at the Kassam Stadium with Alan Fettis taken off injured and Paul Musselwhite deputising in goal. In City's next home game the doubters re-emerged when City, after taking the lead, found themselves 3-1 down against Cheltenham before showing determination to claw back two goals to force a draw. City were tenth in the early season table but were showing signs of promise and on August Bank Holiday won 2-0 away to Cambridge, following it up with a last minute Stuart Green goal to force victory against Boston at the KC. Further wins over Rochdale and Kidderminster sent City up to second in the table and set up a midweek battle against Swansea, who were top.

The queues outside the KC ensured that the match would suffer a delayed kick-off but when the teams took to the field, City made sure that, unlike so often at Boothferry Park, the team were not going to 'blow it' on big match occasions. City were magnificent against a Swansea side who showed why they were promotion challengers. Ian Ashbee in particular gave a true captain's performance and a goal from Stuart Elliott, a powerful header direct from a corner midway through the first half, gave the Tigers a deserved three points and sent City to the top of the table. City's next game saw a 5-1 victory at Northampton, who were expected to be promotion rivals, and City stayed top until late November by which time City had succumbed to their second league defeat, a result of some comedy defending at Huddersfield in front of 4,000 embarrassed away fans. A hiccup just before Christmas saw further defeats at Bristol Rovers and at home to Mansfield but City beat York away on Boxing Day and then defeated Doncaster at the KC, courtesy of a Jason Price hat-trick.

City briefly regained top spot from Doncaster after winning away at Darlington but lost it when losing at home to Torquay. However, City fans were not fussed where the team finished as long as it was in the top three. City never left the second promotion spot and though the Tigers failed to clinch promotion by drawing with Southend, Macclesfield and Huddersfield, Second Division or League One football was confirmed on a glorious day in the South West when City beat Yeovil 2-1 with goals from Stuart Green and, suitably, Ian Ashbee. Thousands of City fans had followed the team down south and many more watched the game at the Vulcan Arena.

Promotion was a triumph for Peter Taylor. Questions were asked of some of his earlier signings, Daniel Webb and Steve Melton particularly, whilst Damien Delaney looked another poor acquisition. However, when moved from left-back to centre-half, Delaney was a revelation and it was fitting that he became the player of the season and capped the moment with a wonderful goal in the final game of the season, a 3-0 thrashing of Bristol Rovers.

Promotion was also a triumph for Adam Pearson. Few would have been surprised if the chairman had wondered what he had let himself in for after seeing both Little and Molby buy in lots of new players only to see the team under-perform on the pitch. However, after a rocky beginning, Pearson had chosen the right man for the job and Taylor led the team to their first promotion in 18 years.

LOOK BACK IN AMBER

Justin Whittle, the last player to be associated with the 'great escape' season, left the Tigers in the close season, joining Grimsby Town whilst another long-server, Paul Musselwhite, returned to former club Scunthorpe. Coming in were Leon Cort, Roland Edge, Aaron Wilbraham, Michael Keane and Delroy Facey. They were joined of course by Hull-born Nick Barmby. There had been rumours all summer long that Barmby was to join his home-town club but it still seemed a fantasy to many. Though he was undergoing a nightmare at Elland Road, he was still good enough for the Championship, if not the Premiership, and signing him was a sign that City were not looking to consolidate on their first season back in League One.

City got off to a good start, beating Bournemouth 1-0 at the KC in the first game, and were third in the table after beating Barnsley at Oakwell courtesy of a late Michael Keane goal with the badge-kissing player seemingly desperate to become a City legend. A home defeat against Bradford was followed by the obligatory heavy defeat at Huddersfield. City were fourth by the time of the Brentford home game which was won 2-0 and the Tigers then embarked on an incredible run of form, winning nine games in a row, eight in the league with City top of the table by the time we won 3-1 away at Stockport.

That run saw City beat Sheffield Wednesday 4-2 at Hillsborough in one of the most memorable away games witnessed by City fans in many years, with about 8,000 away supporters there to witness the performance. Two games later, the Tigers defeated promotion rivals Tranmere 6-1 at the KC thanks mainly to ex-Tiger Theo Whitmore who volunteered to go in goal after Rovers' two keepers were injured during the first half. Thankfully, ex-City manager Brian Little accepted Theo's offer and he conceded five second-half goals. Specially memorable was a twice-taken Stuart Elliott penalty with the City player blasting it into the centre of the goal both times, with Whitmore barely moving in goal, just standing there and watching the ball go past him. Hilarious.

A sticky spell in January and early February with two defeats and two draws gave hope to Tranmere and Sheffield Wednesday, both eyeing City's second place, but a 3-1 defeat of Rovers at Prenton Park re-established the Tigers in the driving seat and further victories over Hartlepool, Torquay and Bournemouth, 4-0 away, gave the Tigers invaluable breathing space.

Tranmere kept on winning and, with City playing Bradford on the Sunday, won their game on Saturday to put them seven points behind us. If we'd have lost at Bradford, Tranmere could have gone four points behind us by winning their game in hand. However, their hopes were finally crushed by a superb professional City display at Valley Parade. Elliott and Barmby scored the goals to virtually secure City's second successive promotion in front of thousands of City fans, who outsang and almost outnumbered the home fans.

It wasn't quite revenge for the end of season game nine years earlier, but it felt good to be overtaking Bradford and so clearly going in the right direction after the dreadful dark days of the Nineties.

A week later promotion was confirmed when, despite missing a last-minute penalty, City drew 0-0 with Swindon and Tranmere's similar result at Blackpool meant that City had been promoted twice in successive seasons, a memorable achievement.

Two promotions in two years and these are good times for those of us who have stayed with the club throughout the last 30 odd years. It's gratifying that success does come to those who wait and to go from relief that the club is still here, to the sight of watching the Tigers stepping out on equal footing against Leeds, Ipswich, Wolves and Sheffield United, is wonderful.

We have been lucky. If things had been different, with different people at the club we could have been looking forward to a season of Conference football at the Boulevard rather than Championship football at one of the best grounds outside the Premiership.

I doubt whether those who became accustomed to great Boothferry Park games in the Sixties would have envisaged the club being locked out of the ground and in danger of falling out the league. Yet it happened and could conceivably happen again, so those who have followed the club through thick and thin will never take seasons like the last two for granted.

Many of those who left the club under a cloud are back and truly happy to see the club run in the way it is today. John Cooper has been with City most of the time, leaving for a couple of years when the club was in the hands of David Lloyd. He's thrilled to see the club in the state it's in today, saying: *'After all that's happened we're here (in the KC Stadium) and that's why I get a little bit annoyed now when we play Peterborough on the back of eight straight wins, leading 2-1 and the fans start booing. People should never forget those days.'*

Tom Wilson kept coming back to the club after his sacking and for him, a man who has become a firm supporter of the Tigers, the club has never been in better hands. He is also back at the club, in yet another capacity: *'One day I was doing something at a local game at Hull and I saw Adam Pearson and John Holmes and they offered me a job here as a matchday host. He said that it had been done at Leeds, a lot of other big clubs were doing it and he wanted to introduce it here. So I said I'd give it a try, I quite enjoyed it and I've been doing it ever since. So I'm there on Saturdays in the boardroom and I still enjoy it and these are great people to work with. John and Adam have time for everybody, they're very professional. They've been there; seen how it should be done and brought those working conditions here to Hull City.*

'Adam is similar to Don Robinson in a way in as much as he will not spend the supporters' money if he doesn't think it is the right thing to do. Much as he backs his manager 100%, whether he agrees or disagrees with who the manager fancies, he backs him and continues to back him, though not to the detriment of the club going into financial difficulties again. It is so good to see somebody at the top again who spends wisely, with supporters in mind. No bragging, claiming the club will do this or that. No boasting, they just get on with the job of making the club a success. They are so professional, they really are.

'We're one of very few clubs which has never been to Wembley or the Millennium Stadium in play-offs or in an LDV Trophy. Sadly in Hull there are still people hanging onto the Chelsea game when they nearly beat Chelsea in 1966, but that's 40 years ago. So the supporters, hopefully, have so much to look forward to in the near future and I think that's why they are backing the present regime because they know they are honest, know that they are far-sighted in that they are looking towards the top division, and why shouldn't we be in a city of this size?

BACK WHERE WE BELONG

'The supporters are so loyal but there are still plenty to come back and who's to say if we are challenging near the top of the Championship, we might well get to 30,000. I don't often go into town but when I do it's unusual for me not to be stopped by people who want to talk about the club. It's great to hear that and I'm pleased that people still talk to me about City. Hopefully part of that is that I didn't run the club down when I was sacked. I still supported the club.

Garreth Roberts also has a matchday role at the club and marvels at the new ground and the fanbase which the club now enjoys: *'You look at the place now (KC Stadium) and it's brilliant that the club is back to where we were at that time, the old Second Division, now the Championship. We took it for granted in those days. We had a good team, good work ethic etc, but we didn't really get the crowds. The people always used to say to me that if the club ever got promoted from the Fourth to the Third and so on the crowds would come back, but to be honest they didn't really grow that much. Even in the Second Division they weren't anything like they are now. It's great to see the club back to where it was and hopefully it'll keep on improving.'*

Don Robinson, who helped keep the club alive in the Eighties, is thrilled that the club is now back into the old Second Division after so much happened to the club since he was chairman: *'Lloyd would have closed the club down and sold the land off, it was just that the council sold the telephone company, so they had money to burn and City had the new stadium built and it all worked out with Adam coming in. I've only been once, to the opening game against Sunderland, but it's marvellous. It's all happening there and it's great. It's got Hull some tremendous national publicity.'*

Several times I've wondered how David Lloyd feels about events at City since he left. He's been strangely silent apart from one quote, naturally giving himself more than a little credit for the state of the club today: *'I got out too early and decided there were better things for me to be doing. A club such as Hull in the Premier League could get 40,000 or more attending each week. And now they have a fantastic stadium and a great team. But they'd still be in a broken down stadium if I hadn't got involved. I was just two or three years too early with my plan.'*

LOOK BACK IN AMBER

I haven't spent too much time on the last couple of seasons but not because I revel in disappointment and trauma. It's a wonderful time to be a City fan and nobody has enjoyed seeing the club succeed more than me. However, the Pearson era is an ongoing story and who knows what the club can achieve over the next few years with Pearson as chairman and Taylor as manager.

I started supporting the club as a seven-year-old with the club getting big crowds in a marvellous stadium with an exciting team on the field heading towards the First Division. Over thirty years later I bring my seven-year-old son over to Hull for him to see big crowds in a marvellous stadium with an exciting team on the field. It's almost as if the last thirty or so years have never *happened*!